Elizabeth W. (Elizabeth Williams) Champney

Three Vassar Girls at Home

A Holiday Trip of three College Girls through the South and West. Vol. 1

Elizabeth W. (Elizabeth Williams) Champney

Three Vassar Girls at Home
A Holiday Trip of three College Girls through the South and West. Vol. 1

ISBN/EAN: 9783337147358

Printed in Europe, USA, Canada, Australia, Japan

Cover: Foto ©Andreas Hilbeck / pixelio.de

More available books at **www.hansebooks.com**

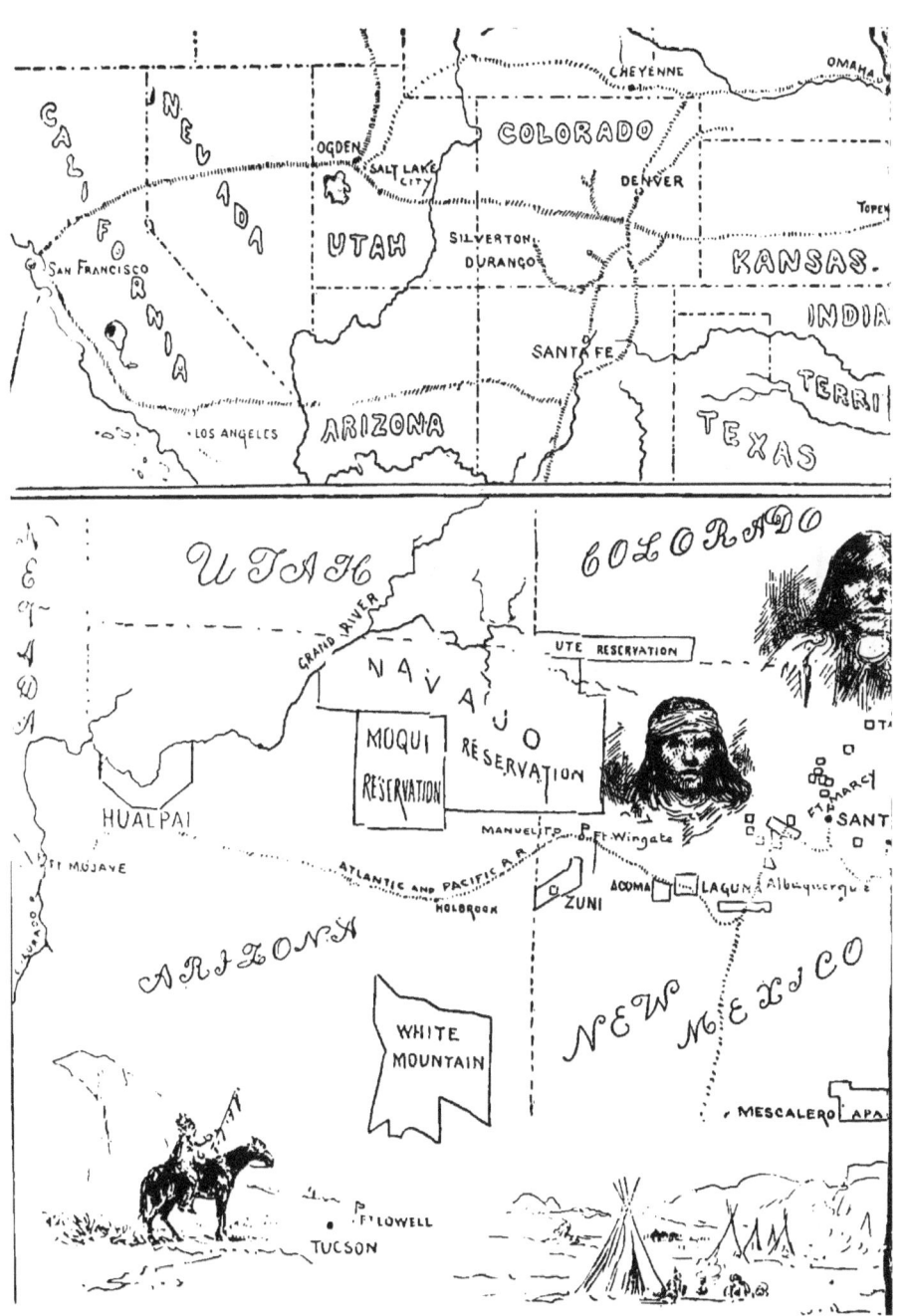

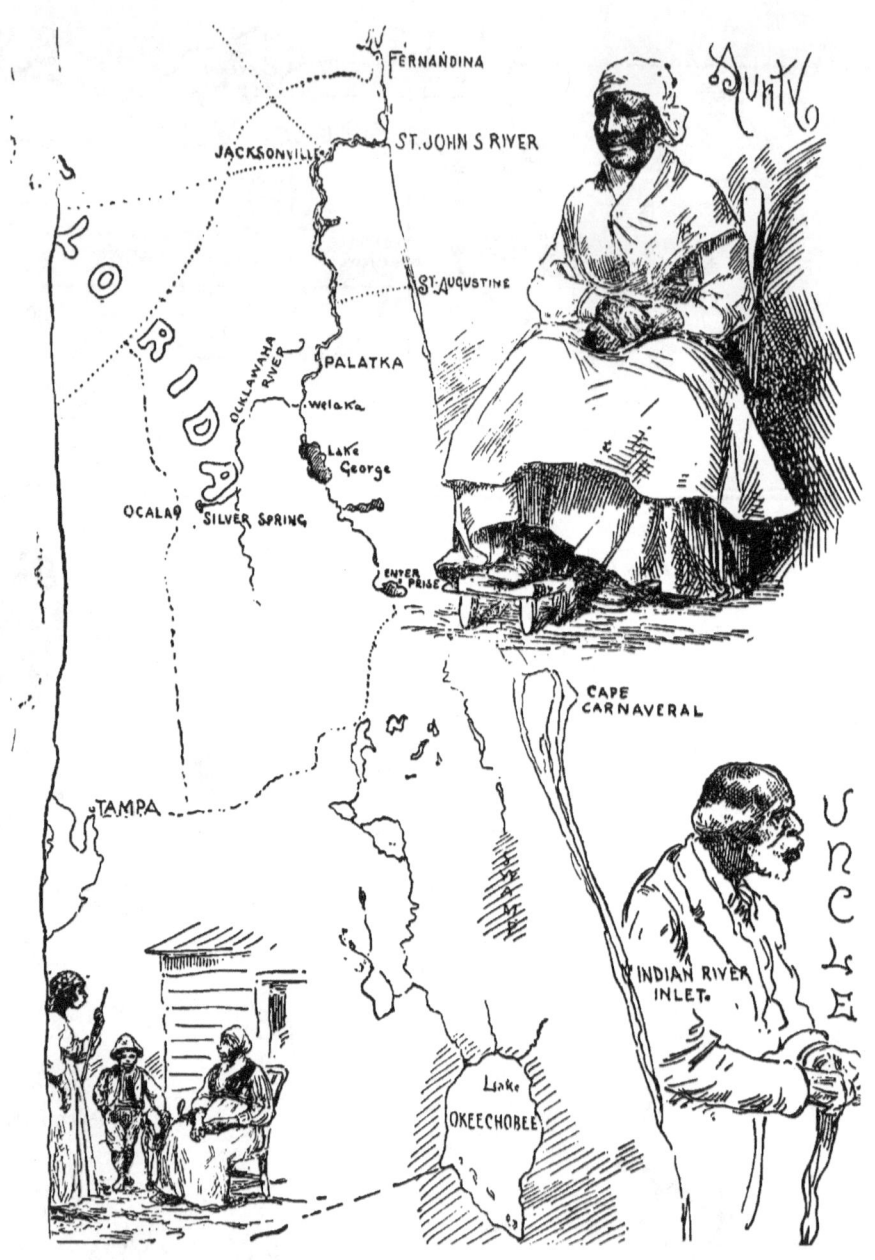

ON THE OCKLAWAHA.

Three Vassar Girls
At Home

A HOLIDAY TRIP OF THREE COLLEGE GIRLS

THROUGH THE SOUTH AND WEST

BY

LIZZIE W. CHAMPNEY

ILLUSTRATED BY "CHAMP" AND OTHERS

BOSTON
ESTES AND LAURIAT, PUBLISHERS
301-305 Washington Street
1888

CONTENTS.

Chapter
- I. Unpicturesque America
- II. St. Augustine . .
- III. Leaves of Palm .
- IV. Human Nature
- V. Sweet and Sour Oranges . . . .
- VI. The Captain's Wager and the Doctor's Revenge
- VII. Up the Ocklawaha . .
- VIII. A Camp-Meeting and a Great Emergency
- IX. In the Furnace .
- X. Crossing the Bridge
- XI. Wild Colorado
- XII. The Rockies and Salt Lake
- XIII. Camping on the Yellowstone . .
- XIV. California and Arizona
- XV. The Pueblos . . . .
- XVI. Taken Prisoner . . . .

ILLUSTRATIONS.

	PAGE
On the Ocklawaha . . . . . *Frontispiece*	
Madeleine	12
Cleo writes to her Father . . .	13
A Florida Landscape	14
"Fond of dress or flirtation"	18
Aunt Pen and Madeleine	21
On the Hotel Piazza, St. Augustine .	24
Dr. Pettyman	25
"I 'se gwine ress, I is"	30
Captain Saunters	31
An Afternoon Drive	32
Heron	35
Yulee Ponce	37
Oriental Palm	39
"The Critter"	42
The Camp in the Forest .	43
Death of Turf .	47
On the Veranda	51
Entrance to the Old Fort	53
An Episode in the Seminole War .	57
One of Geronimo's Band	60
The Old Gate, St. Augustine . . .	61
Mr. Tait and his Guests	63
The Sour-Orange Man . . .	64
Old Spanish House	65
Captain Saunters calls	67
The Watch-Tower	69
Flamingoes	71
Pelicans fishing	77
"The Critter" spins a Yarn	79
The Frog and the Snipe	81

	PAGE
"As they drifted back by sunset"	85
Her Favorite Book	86
Cleopatra and the Captain .	89
A well-remembered Hat . . .	93
Floating Alligator Island . .	95
A Cypress Swamp . . .	99
A Florida Type	101
"Too well-to-do for exertion" .	102
Silver Spring in Former Times	103
The Sweet-Orange Man . .	105
At the Camp-Meeting	108
"Wriggling out from under a mass of tree-roots"	111
Flying Squirrels . . .	115
The Justice of the Peace	118
Cathedral at St. Augustine	127
"Turning, she saw Captain Saunters" .	128
"A sphinx in spectacles" . .	129
"A tall angel stood beneath it" .	132
Feeding the Chickens	137
A Shambling Negro	138
In the Hammock . .	141
The Bridge	144
Pier of Brooklyn Bridge	146
Gateway to the Garden of the Gods .	149
Columns of Red Sandstone	151
"She has lived in Leadville ever since it was projected"	152
A Colorado Savage	152
"That 's a Redfern jacket" . . .	153
The Latest English Style	154

ILLUSTRATIONS.

	PAGE
A Street in Leadville	155
Ah Lee	159
A Dangerous Ride	161
Cañon of the Arkansas	165
Miss Hurlburt	169
The Cowboy	170
The Minister	170
The Senator	170
"Long snow-sheds which protect the track"	171
The Mormon Tabernacle	173
Little Swedish Girl	175
A Latter-Day Saint	176
A Pioneer's Home	177
Dick and his Family	180
Crater of "Old Faithful"	181
The Geyser Land	184
The Grotto	185
"Yulee and Madeleine were both fond of fishing"	188
A Cascade in the Yellowstone Park	190
Map	192
In the Grand Cañon	194
The Yosemite Valley	197
One of the Big Trees	199
Tranquil Mirror Lake	201
Mother Flanagan	203
Grand Cañon, looking East	204
A Zuñi Indian	206
The Nevada Fall in the Yosemite	207
Madeleine and "He-wants-to-know"	210
Indian Reservations	213
A Zuñi Village	217
The Major	219
A Room in the Pueblo of Acoma	221
The Interpreter	224
Ancient Pueblo restored	227
Mr. Hurlburt as a Prospector	229
Watching a Pueblo Dance	231

THREE VASSAR GIRLS AT HOME.

THREE VASSAR GIRLS AT HOME.

CHAPTER I.

UNPICTURESQUE AMERICA.

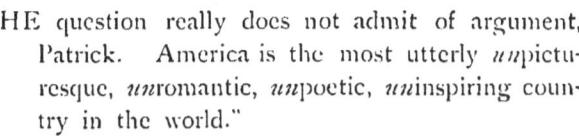HE question really does not admit of argument, Patrick. America is the most utterly *un*picturesque, *un*romantic, *un*poetic, *un*inspiring country in the world."

The young lady addressed as Patrick — Miss Cleopatra Atchison, a younger sister of Barbara Atchison, with whom many of our readers are acquainted — looked up quickly with some bright reply trembling on her pouting lips; but her friend was not ready to listen.

"I confess, Cleo dear," she said, "that your opinion ought to have a showing; but I have not nearly expressed mine as yet. America has no background. I felt that when I was in England. We have no castles, cathedrals, abbeys, or history, — no knights in armor or troubadours. No wonder that there is no spirit of chivalry in our modern life; that American men are a mere sordid drove of money-getters, and American women loud, shallow, and pretentious."

"Madeleine, Madeleine," protested Patrick warmly, a spot of bright color burning in each cheek, "you are carrying the matter entirely too far. You don't mean what you say. All American men are not mercenary wretches. To be particular, there is my father; as knightly a heart throbs under his U. S. brass buttons as ever beat 'neath a coat of mail; and you certainly do not include your mother in your sweeping category."

MADELEINE.

Madeleine's face softened ; her mother was the only person whom she passionately loved. It was for her sake that she had relinquished her ambition to graduate at the head of her class, and was now, in the middle of her senior year, packing her trunks for Florida. Mrs. Morse was recovering from an attack of pneumonia, and her physician had recommended Florida for the remainder of the winter. When Madeleine heard of this decision she instantly decided that it was her duty to accompany her mother. And when her father had replied that this was not necessary, — for though he could not leave his business to accompany his wife, Uncle Jonah was going to Florida on business, and Aunt Pen would accompany them and care for the invalid, — Madeleine was more than ever confirmed in her decision.

"Aunt Pen will *kill* mother in ten days," she explained to her friend. "She is the greatest talker on this continent; unless I am there to protect mother, her trip will do her no good."

"And what will become of your college course?" asked Madeleine.

"I shall study while I am away, and be back for the spring examinations. If I pass, well and good; if not, I'll graduate next year. You will be valedictorian, Pat, and I shall be on hand with plenty of bouquets at Commencement Day. But how I shall miss you all next year! I wish you would take a post-graduate course."

Cleopatra's cheeks glowed, but she said nothing; and yet she was a girl of sudden impulses, and on lesser occasions than these had been exuberant in her sympathy. She retired to her own room shortly after, and busied herself in writing a long letter to her father.

It was a week after the announcement of Mrs. Morse's illness that Madeleine was to start on her Southern journey. Cleopatra had been full of a repressed impatience. A strange restlessness possessed the girl; her studies were neglected, and she held long consultations with the Lady Principal. She took a lively interest in Madeleine's plans, reading or rather skimming all the books on Florida which the library afforded, and talking them over with her friend, who persisted in not being interested in her proposed trip except as it was to affect her mother's health.

CLEO WRITES TO HER FATHER.

Cleopatra spent much of her time during the last two days in packing her own trunk, much to Madeleine's surprise, for it lacked a week of the holidays. She was always in time and waiting for the distribution of letters, and there was a settled look of disappointment on her face after they were given out. She acted, in short, like a girl with a secret on her mind; and when Madeleine taxed her with this she replied, "My dear, I've two of them, and they are just devouring me." Then, to beat off Madeleine's inquiries, she launched once more into their staple discussion on the merits of American scenery.

"I think our country is the most picturesque in the world," she said. "Just wait till I get you out among our Colorado mountains; if you are not more deeply moved than you ever were by any foreign minster, I am mistaken. And as for this Florida trip which you profess to scorn, I fancy it will waken in you an entirely new appreciation of your native land."

"Perhaps so," Madeleine admitted languidly. "If we could only take it alone, — just you and I together, Pat, — and could float away in a canoe up some unexplored river, like Ponce de Leon, — that would

A FLORIDA LANDSCAPE.

be worth while; but to be dragged about by Uncle Jonah and Aunt Pen in a parlor car from one fashionable resort to another, with anxiety for mother tugging at my heart-strings, and the thought of you finishing your course triumphantly at this dear old college — Oh, Cleo, it is almost more than I can bear."

Madeleine never called her friend Cleo except when profoundly moved; and as she buried her face in her Moral Philosophy, Cleopatra sprang to her side, — her secret was almost out. But at that instant the corridor teacher tapped at the door. "A telegram for Miss Atchison!"

Cleopatra snatched it from that admirable lady's hand, and tore it quite in two, in her eagerness to open the envelope. She glanced at only the first two words, and then, unmindful of the stupefaction of the gentle corridor teacher, "Glory!" she shouted. "Madeleine, I'm going too."

"What do you mean?" asked the bewildered girl. "You are not going to give up graduating this year; your father will never consent."

"Yes, he will; he has. He'd rather I would stay East longer,— you see, he doesn't know what to do with me after I come home; and I wrote him that I had a cough,— I truly have, a little one,— and that I was afraid I wouldn't pass, and all that, and I couldn't graduate without you. Madeleine dear, we *will* finish this year, after all, for we will study together and recite to each other, and astonish all the professors and all the girls by walking right over their heads when it comes to examination — Oh, Miss Meecher, excuse me; I didn't mean to bump against you;" for in her ecstasy Cleopatra had waltzed Madeleine around the table, and whirled her madly against the little corridor teacher, who, finding that a withering glance had no effect, now retired with mingled dignity and expedition, while the girls paced the corridor with more sobriety. "That's secret No. 2, Madeleine; No. 1 you shall know sometime. What glorious times we will have!"

"I am glad you are going," Madeleine replied, much touched by her friend's devotion; "but you will find it very stupid."

"No fears of that! I'll take my camera; I have always wanted to see more of the East before I go home."

"I don't believe you will find a mortal thing worth photographing. If we were going down the Rhine or through Switzerland, what a lovely album you could make! I had a friend who illustrated "Hare's Walks in Rome" by inserting photographs of all the places mentioned, and another who took Irving's "Tales of the Alhambra" to

Granada and treated it in the same way; but Florida scenery is notoriously flat and uninteresting. I really don't see why you have decided to go."

"You are tired out, Madeleine, and the trip is sure to do you good; and you've only to provide yourself with some good books to have an ever-open door of escape from boredom of every kind."

"There it is again! What books shall we take? The novels are as bad as real people. What has become, Pat, of the old ideals of high thought and noble endeavor? Even the novels are prosaic and commonplace, and we have green-grocers and restaurant clerks for heroes, and the silliest or most vapid of heroines."

"It seems to me," said Cleopatra, thoughtfully, "that you misunderstand the purpose of the realistic school of writers. They cannot intend to drag our ideals in the mire. I think they intend to show us the nobility and pathos, the heroism and self-sacrifice, that exist unsuspected right in this commonness with which we are surrounded."

"It is well disguised, then," Madeleine replied, with something like a sneer. "I would never suspect our popular authors of any such motive, and the greatest fault which I have to find with them is that their characters are so aggravatingly real. They are exactly like the people we meet every day. Howells's women are precisely the women who exasperate me so much, his conversations just what one overhears in the street-cars and between the acts at the matinées. Oh, I am sick of it all, and hungry to see one really grand life, not all sham and hollowness!"

"Perhaps you will find it in Florida, Madeleine, hidden away in the pine barrens or in the everglades, near to Nature's heart,—a character like the Sir Galahad of that little anonymous novel that you liked so much."

"Yes; that was a really natural, simple soul, and yet so true and great. There were many unusual thoughts in that book. I wonder who wrote it?"

"Some one quite unknown to fame, I've no doubt. It is probably a first attempt, and not likely to be followed up by another; for I hear the book is not over-successful, in spite of the send-off you gave it in your book review in the Miscellany."

"I might have known that such a book would not be successful," Madeleine replied musingly. "Who is there to care for it in our driving, pushing, hurrying, scurrying America?" The girl frowned as she spoke, so savagely that a friend who caught her glance at the end of the corridor wondered what she had done to offend her, and reported to another acquaintance that Madeleine Morse was "mad" with her, and she believed "that snoopy Cleopatra Atchison" had told her something to her disadvantage.

Meantime the two girls continued their walk up and down the long corridor, chatting of their projected trip and always in the same tone, — Patrick light and joyous, Madeleine cavilling now at the scenery and now at the people of her native country. And yet the girl's nature was not sour or discontented. She was only undeveloped and inexperienced. Her soul was full of noble aspirations and high ideals; her heart bursting with a craving for the beautiful in Nature, art, and, above all, in human life. This craving had been stimulated by a course of unusual study, into which she had thrown herself with high enthusiasm. Each vacation she had left her books unwillingly, to be taken by her family to the different watering-places to meet only the fashionable class of city people, — women who were fond of dress or flirtation, dancing young men, middle-aged men whose entire existence could be covered by a trade-dollar, and girls whom she despised for their frivolity. Because she had visited a number of these watering-places, she fancied that her experience was wider than it really was, not reflecting that at her home in New York, Saratoga, Newport, and Cape May she had seen only one class of people, and that a limited one. Her mother she excepted from her sweeping category. Mrs. Morse had a fine, elevated nature like her daughter's; but maternal

duties had absorbed her, and she had laid aside all other aspirations to become an excellent mother of a large brood of little children. She sympathized with her eldest daughter, but never tried to prove that her theories were wrong. When Aunt Pen, Mrs. Morse's more worldly sister, argued with her, Mrs. Morse sometimes admitted that Madeleine's views of life might change if she were once happily married, and at other times took the girl's part, asserting that she had known many single women who really seemed happy, and that

"FOND OF DRESS OR FLIRTATION."

Madeleine should be left perfectly free to choose her own career in life. Aunt Pen had no patience with her sister. "The girl will be an old maid," she lamented, as though this were the crowning misfortune which could ever befall a woman. "She will certainly be an old maid unless Providence interferes to prevent;" and Aunt Pen made an inward resolution that Providence should interfere.

To a certain extent her designs were favored. Uncle Jonah, Aunt Pen's husband, had lands in Florida which he thought needed attention; and as Mrs. Morse's married daughter was spending the winter at home, and was an excellent housekeeper, she was free to make the trip deemed so necessary for her health. Mrs. Morse would not have allowed Madeleine to make this sacrifice for her comfort, had not Aunt Pen persuaded her that the girl was herself overworked and nervously overwrought, and that the change would be extremely beneficial for her. In her inmost soul Aunt Pen saw in this circumstance the interposition of Providence which she had hoped for, and determined that this season should mark, as indeed it did, a turning-point in Madeleine's life. As for this Western friend who desired to make the trip with them before returning to some frontier post, Aunt Pen saw in her a valuable ally. "Those Western girls are always jolly and good company," she thought to herself; "she will attract just the desirable individuals, and when once brought into our circle I can easily divert the one I approve of to Madeleine. She will help keep Madeleine good-natured, instead of moping like a tombstone, and lead her into all sorts of gayeties which the girl would never consent to were she alone. Altogether, it is a very good idea to take this Atchison girl along. Madeleine is a classic beauty, and has perfect breeding; the Atchison girl will have Western manners, just a little loud: Madeleine is an heiress; the Atchison girl is sure to be poor,— altogether an admirable foil for Madeleine."

Then Uncle Jonah handed Aunt Pen a letter postmarked St. Augustine, and that estimable lady read with great satisfaction, —

"The greatest catch of the season is Captain Saunters; he is the only son of the senior member of the firm of Saunters & Scuter, who made such a fortune in wheel-grease. He is a universal favorite, and a little spoiled, of course."

Aunt Pen folded the letter and put aside her eyeglasses. "Jonah," said she, "we must make St. Augustine our first stop. Have you telegraphed for rooms? We shall want to stay a fortnight."

"But, my dear, you know I want to go up the Ocklawaha at once."

"Certainly; but I've been thinking there must be a great deal of malaria and alligators and things on the Ocklawaha, and it would never do to take Miranda and those girls into such a dangerous region."

"As you please," said Uncle Jonah, with gentle resignation. "I can make the trip alone; but you miss it. It's the prettiest part of Florida."

Meantime the friends were on their way to New York. "Just think," said Cleopatra, looking out from the car window upon the frozen Hudson, "how soon we shall exchange this snowy landscape for palmettoes and 'the banana with leaf like a tent'!"

"If we could only go camping in the wilds with Uncle Jonah!" said Madeleine; "but Aunt will take us to the most fashionable hotels, and to the same imbecile young men who imagine themselves so extremely irresistible."

Patrick laughed gayly. "I don't see why we should concern ourselves about the young men," she replied. "They rather amuse me, but they never trouble me long; I have only to pretend that I am preternaturally learned, and they flee from me in terror."

"Do they?" asked Madeleine. "I will buy a pair of blue spectacles at once, and stalk about with a microscope under one arm and a Greek lexicon under the other. But, Pat, you don't know my Aunt Pen; she is the most irrepressible matchmaker. She has married all her daughters, and nearly all of my cousins as well. Her only unsuccessful financiering attempt was with little Myrtle; she whisked her off to Italy, and nearly had her wedded to an Italian Count, when some way, no one knows how, the child managed to show a little courage and to resist her machinations until, by the aid of a good fairy, the Count was proved to be a swindler. I am Aunt Pen's despair. She knows that I am a man-hater, and it fills her with horror to think that one of her nieces has voluntarily elected to be an old maid. She has labored with mother on her folly in allowing me to come to Vassar, where she thinks my unnatural notions have been confirmed. I have no doubt that she is revolving some deep-laid scheme for disposing of us both in the matrimonial market."

AUNT PEN AND MADELEINE.

"She has very short time for her schemes," demurred Cleopatra; "we are not likely to be deeply entangled."

"Trust Aunt Pen for that; she's a lightning-calculator. She took Cousin Sophy for a week to Lake Mohonk, and had her engaged to an oil-merchant thirty minutes before the time was up."

"Well, Madeleine, if your gentle Cousin Myrtle could resist her machinations when a foreign nobleman was in question, I think that you and I will be tolerably safe. I shall take my camera and devote myself to taking instantaneous views; and if any rash young man approaches you, I will point it at him, and you shall see how quickly he will take himself from the scene. I do not think your Aunt Pen will attempt to make any plans for my future, but if she does I expect to have great fun in frustrating them. I am not afraid of young men, Madeleine dear; I was brought up in the army."

"*Afraid* of them!" Madeleine's lip took a contemptuous curl; it was as if she had said, "I am not afraid of a blue-bottle fly."

CHAPTER II.

ST. AUGUSTINE.

First Impressions.

HE quaint half-foreign city lay basking in the sun, its foreignness almost blotted out by the mushroom growth of gigantic hotels and an overwhelming tide of pleasure-and-health-seeking Northerners. It took a keen eye, alert for the picturesque, to detect the old coquina houses, with the gray arches of their inner patios rendered more shadowy by palms and cascades of cloth-of-gold roses; for these old landmarks were being rapidly shouldered aside and even displaced by pretentious villas. But old Castle San Marco slumbered still just outside the town, and the tide lapped its walls as it did in the old days of Spanish occupation, while the ever-encroaching sand-dune strove to bury the fortress with its legends of horror out of men's minds and sight. From the hotel piazza the wide-sweeping bay could be seen shimmering sleepily in the sunshine, just as though it were not January and storms were vexing the northern seas. Everything suggested lazy day-dreams and the land where it is always afternoon. Madeleine, with an expression of unwonted interest in her weary face, looked from the omnibus that rattled briskly across the long causeway that crosses the Maria Sanchez River. A crack of the whip, and the Spanish Plaza was in view,

and she heard the unmusical bells of the cathedral clanging the hour discordantly from their bizarre arches. They passed down St. George's Street, lined with its picturesque booths and curiosity shops, to the hotel, whose gleaming whiteness Willis would have described as a Mont Blanc hotel with Dover cliff verandas.

ON THE HOTEL PIAZZA, ST. AUGUSTINE.

A ragged negro boy in a Tam-o'-Shanter cap was wandering through the halls, seeking a purchaser for the yellow jasmine with which his arms were filled. Madeleine untangled the long sprays with rapture; the faint but exquisite odor reminded her of nothing she had ever met with, for no perfume is so delicately sweet as that of the jasmine. She fastened a knot of it in her mother's dress, and engaged the boy to bring her some every day of their stay.

That evening, after Mrs. Morse was comfortably settled, the girls strolled out with Uncle Jonah to visit the shops. They were so oddly un-American that Madeleine was reminded, in spite of herself, of walks in Nice and Florence, of booths along the quays and the tiny jewelry-stores of the Palais Royal and the Rue de Rivoli. Still, these were more Spanish in character. The street was very narrow and overhung with gayly painted balconies, which jutted from the upper stories of the yellowish white and whity-gray coquina-built houses. It only needed a black-mantillaed beauty leaning over the balustrade, and gayer trappings on the mules which threaded their way beneath, to complete the illusion and reproduce Fontarabia or Seville.

"It is a pity," said Madeleine, "that the costumes are not Spanish. See that dapper little fellow coming down the street, his slim little legs in very tight pantaloons, and his entire figure only a trifle less slender than his rattan; how utterly insignificant he looks!"

"Who? What?" asked Uncle Jonah, vaguely; and then, catching sight of the individual in question, he exclaimed, "Why, it is Dr. Pettyman!"

DR. PETTYMAN.

Dr. Pettyman approached on hearing his name called in so hearty a tone, and, recognizing Uncle Jonah through his lorgnette, bowed with great affability, while Uncle Jonah presented his friend to the young ladies, launching, in his desire to say something agreeable, into one of his not unusual malapropisms: "They were just talking about you, my dear fellow; indeed they were."

"Deeply honored, I am sure," murmured the gentleman. "And what were they saying?"

"My niece was just saying — Upon my soul, what *were* you saying, Madeleine?" exclaimed Uncle Jonah, suddenly realizing that her remark would not bear repetition.

Madeleine replied, with heightened color, that it was hardly necessary to increase Dr. Pettyman's vanity by repeating their remarks; and passing her hand through her uncle's arm, she left the task of entertaining the Doctor to Cleopatra. As they fell behind on the narrow sidewalk, Cleopatra remarked that they had just been saying it was such a pity that there was no foreign population to enhance the quaintness of the Spanish surroundings.

"But there is a distinct foreign population," replied Dr. Pettyman, "very interesting to an ethnologist. These shops are kept principally by Minorcans. Seduced by false promises from their Mediterranean island, the Minorcan colony were held for many years to the cultivation of indigo, in a slavery more degrading if possible than that of the negro; and their descendants still suffer from this heritage of servitude."

Theoretically Dr. Pettyman pitied the Minorcans; practically he considered them a low set, and their social ostracism quite the correct thing.

They had been walking so near together that Madeleine had overheard the conversation, and was interested in spite of herself. A group of young Minorcan girls now passed them, bareheaded, with olive complexions and melting Italian eyes; they were plaiting palmetto braids as they walked, and they called each other soft Southern names, — "Maruja," "Manuela."

Madeleine now read the names upon the signs more carefully, — Carreras, Oliveras, Pacetti; and she drew her uncle into a wee sparrow-box of a shop which displayed the sign, "Miss Ponce, Palm Work."

"I wonder whether she is a relative of Ponce de Leon," she remarked.

"Ask her," said Uncle Jonah, heartily. "See here, Miss," he added, before his niece could restrain him, addressing a slender girl with short, dark, curling hair who came forward to receive them; "my niece thinks you may be a relation of a friend of hers."

"Oh no, Uncle. Ponce de Leon is not an acquaintance of mine;" and seeing that the girl's eyes were smiling, Madeleine's mirth overcame her vexation, and she laughed merrily. Miss Ponce showed them her collection,—tinted palm-leaf fans, and a large collection of doll's hats. A quantity of dried grasses, the downy Occola plume, silky thistle-balls, sprays of sea-oats, ferns, and the gray Spanish moss decorated the little shop. But what interested Cleopatra most was an album of sea-weed which Miss Ponce brought forward unasked, and laid before Dr. Pettyman, quite as if he were in the habit of calling at the shop especially with a view to looking over this collection.

"There are some new Callithamnions," she said, pointing to some beautiful crimson mosses, "to the which you are quite welcome if you will serve yourself of them, and some new specimen, to the which I have not written ze name for why I could not find them in ze little book."

Dr. Pettyman tumbled over the leaves of the album rapidly, scribbling a name or two as it seemed to Cleopatra very much at random, and unscrupulously abstracting a number of rare specimens, which he placed carefully in his note-book, and for which he did not offer to pay.

Cleopatra felt like resenting this cool behavior for the young girl when she saw the Doctor appropriate to himself all of the Bryozoons and a pale-green, plumy Ectocarpus tomentosus, the only one in the collection. Miss Ponce seemed to consider the naming of her unknown varieties recompense enough; but what weakened this consideration with Cleopatra was a haunting suspicion that the Doctor's science was sometimes at fault. There was a flippant readiness with which he dealt out his long names which convinced her that there was something of the quack in his make-up. But then Cleopatra was given to jumping at conclusions with too few data, and had sometimes formed violent prejudices on insufficient grounds. She had never made a specialty of this department of botany, and could not meet the Doctor on his own ground; but she knew that Madeleine was perfectly able to do so, and she now asked her opinion as to a sea-weed which resembled a spray of feathery asparagus, which the Doctor had called a Bryopsis. Madeleine unhesitatingly pronounced it Cladophora flexuosa, but started as she did so; for the truth was that Madeleine had not been thinking of sea-weed at all. She had been studying the young girl's face, making herself acquainted with a new type, and she had never before realized how interesting *people* could be.

Yulee Ponce was a Minorcan by descent; but the strain had refined itself through each generation, and something distinctively American had been infused, unconsciously breathed in with the atmosphere in which she lived. Heredity was proclaimed by the mellow, halting English, so charming in its accent and in its very faultiness, by her languid Southern movements and the melting depths of her glorious Mediterranean eyes, — eyes which spoke at once of Spain or Italy or Greece. But her form had not the voluptuous roundness of her race: she was slight, almost spare; her face had a pathetic expression; a pallor in the complexion, a quiver about the mouth, and a hungry yearning in her eyes told of meagre fare for mind and body, of a great longing for opportunities just beyond her reach.

Dr. Pettyman flushed when he saw that Madeleine was an adept in obscure botany, and edged uneasily to another part of the room with Cleopatra, endeavoring to interest her in sea-beans, which he explained were the fruit of a leguminous plant. These beans drop into the sea on the coasts of the West Indies, and are washed over to Florida by the Gulf Stream. They looked together at different varieties of these, some like cranberries set as earrings, some like mottled agate as sleeve buttons, and the rare, highly polished leopard skins.

Cleopatra, who had taken a violent prejudice to the Doctor, displayed no interest, and that gentleman turned the conversation to her friend. "Miss Morse seems very fond of sea-weed," he said; "we must make up a yachting party of young people, and gather some of the fine varieties which abound here."

"I advise you not to invite Madeleine to such a cruise," Cleopatra replied.

"Am I mistaken in supposing that she is interested in Algæ?"

"No; but she is not interested in gentlemen, and we have both taken a solemn vow to keep out of society and devote ourselves to study while in Florida."

Dr. Pettyman elevated his eyebrows, but did not look as displeased as Cleo wished.

In the mean time Yulee Ponce, always alert where her beloved Algæ were concerned, had noticed that Madeleine had spoken with the familiarity and positiveness of an expert. "You have studied ze sea-weed," she said timidly; "you do zen lof zem."

"Yes," Madeleine replied with a smile; "I do indeed love them, and you have a very fine collection. I would like to buy a set of you, and I would be so glad if you would let me go with you sometime in search of them."

The girl's face lighted with pleasure. "Zat would be great honaire," she said; "I haf thought sometime to go by boat of sail to Anastasia Lighthouse; the water is more stormier, and zere come there some currents which dash on ze rocks some variety we do neffer see on our coast."

"That will make a delightful excursion," said Madeleine; "and meantime I will bring you some books I have on the subject of botany, in which you may be interested."

"Zat will be so fery lofing of you," said the girl, "and I will be of ze greatest care possible, if I may take zem with me while I make a small journey with my muzza for some palm-branch for her work."

their average intellectual abilities by hers. I should enjoy nothing better than to go into a few antiquarian and ethnological researches with you, but they could hardly be comprised within the limits of a single walk. I shall be pleased to call to-morrow afternoon, and would like to be your guide in visiting certain old Spanish houses, not easily accessible to the ordinary tourist. I am an enthusiastic student of Nature, Miss Morse, but I hope to show you how much more interesting a study is human nature."

Madeleine thanked him, and they parted on the hotel veranda. If she could only have seen how the little man's bearing changed after he left her, — how he strutted along the sea-wall until he seemed almost to have grown an inch, and the wide swath he cut as he swished his little rattan from left to right. Clarence Saunters, sitting there in the moonlight, laughed aloud as he saw him coming. "I should be pleased to know what it is which you find so mirth-inspiring," Dr. Pettyman exclaimed, deeply incensed.

"I beg your pardon," Saunters replied, "but you looked so absurdly victorious. Has she accepted you, my good fellow?"

"I'll have you to know, Captain Saunters," replied the Doctor (who thoroughly hated the Captain), still more angered by this chance remark, "that you are not the irresistible lady's man that you think yourself, and that I have the honor of acquaintance with a young lady, Miss Madeleine Morse, who I am willing to wager twenty dollars would not so much as accept an invitation to boat or to an afternoon drive with you."

CAPTAIN SAUNTERS.

"Done!" replied the other, thoughtlessly. "I should like to see the lady who has the poor taste to prefer your attentions to mine; and as I happen to know the aunt of the young person in question, and to have just come from a pleasant chat with her, where she invited me at least three times to call on Miss Madeleine, I think I have a fair chance of winning the wager."

The Doctor's eyes turned positively green; they shone with triumph as well as malice as he thought how easily he would upset

AN AFTERNOON DRIVE.

Captain Saunters's calculations by telling Miss Morse that the young man had betted upon his probable success in her good graces.

"I say, Pettyman," exclaimed Saunters, suddenly. "I can't do it, after all. It isn't a nice thing to make a bet of that kind about a young lady;" and he turned hastily upon his heel.

"Very easy to slip out of it on those grounds," said the Doctor, sneeringly; "but if you are afraid of losing your money—"

"I'm not afraid," Saunters called back, "but I'm off for a few days' shooting;" and he mentally determined not to return until the young lady in question had left St. Augustine.

Aunt Pen met the girls as they entered the hotel. "My dear Madeleine," she murmured, "it is *such* a pity that you have not been at home. I have just met an old acquaintance, a most charming young man, a Captain Clarence Saunters."

Madeleine made a little scornful gesture. "I am not interested in young men," she said.

"And yet," Cleopatra replied a little maliciously, "this unimpressible maiden has just invited a very exquisite young man to call upon her and to act as her guide while in St. Augustine."

Madeleine flushed indignantly. "I never did anything of the kind," she retorted hotly; and then correcting herself added, "Besides, the Doctor is n't a man, he 's only an ethnologist, and we are going to study human nature."

"A very proper study for young ladies," said Aunt Pen, dryly.

CHAPTER III.

LEAVES OF PALM.

"THE girl looks as though she had just stepped from a Florentine altar-piece," thought young Saunters, "or rather as though she were still standing in one." The thought was not an unnatural one, for the two palms grew so near together that their straight trunks formed the sides of a frame, and their curving branches the arch of the top; a sunset sky behind made the beaten gold background for the saintlike figure within. Her tall, slender form was draped in a dark-blue cotton dress, of scant pattern and coarse material, falling in simple straight lines close to the figure; but its meagreness had nothing of the vulgarity of poverty about it, — it only carried out the idea of spirituality, and the eyes were the same appealing ones which had thrilled straight through Madeleine's heart. She held a palm-branch above her head, and Saunters remembered that the palm was the symbol of martyrdom. He had been shooting heron and duck along the river, and had wandered off into the pine-barrens of Florida, and imagined that he was at quite a distance from any human habitation. The facts of the case were that he was lost, having become separated the evening before from his guide, Pedro. He had kindled a fire and slept in the open air, with no other companions than

Turf and Field, his two dogs. He had been walking all the morning with no breakfast, endeavoring to find a way out of the forest, and becoming every moment more hungry and more alarmed. When Yulee turned her Fra Angelico face toward him, though grateful enough to be in a devout frame of mind, his thoughts did not linger in the realms of Florentine Art.

Yulee, with womanly compassion for his famished state, led him at once to a gypsy-like camp at a little distance, where a small tent was pitched, and a bony horse was tethered near a Florida tip-cart. A gaunt man with a not unintelligent face came forward and was introduced as "Meester Raphael Ponce, my fazer." He took Saunters's gun and placed it beside his own near the wagon, but he declined the offer of a share in his game-bag, saying that they had "more duck as zey could shoot in ten day." A fat, swarthy-skinned woman was next presented by Yulee as "my muzza," and immediately returned to her brooding over a little fire of pine knots which snapped cheerily under a tin coffee-pot. The beverage within was a combination of roasted sweet potatoes and chiccory, with a little Rio to give it a flavor; but the aroma which greeted Saunters's fainting senses seemed to him the most delicious he had ever breathed. He munched the

YULEE PONCE.

broiled duck and the "pone" of corn bread, and drank the milkless coffee from a tin cup with intense delight. The wants of his grosser nature having been more completely satisfied with a slice of cold boiled ham, he was prepared to enjoy an unexpected intellectual treat. The little martyr of the palm-branch, as he inwardly called his companion, opened a botanist's can, and began arranging the specimens which she had collected during the day, upon sheets of porous paper, preparatory to pressing them between two small boards, which she compressed tightly by means of a pair of shawl-straps. "We are on a what you call ze expedition for ze botany," she remarked by way of explanation.

"You have studied botany?" asked Saunters; and in spite of himself a slight tone of surprise crept into the question. He was immediately ashamed of his rudeness. If he had taken it for granted that the girl was as untutored as she was unassuming, he need not so obviously have shown his thought.

She replied simply, as though she had not noticed the implication: "Miss Morse is giving me some lesson."

"And who is Miss Morse?" asked Saunters.

"She ees a saint," replied Yulee, reverently.

"A society of saints and martyrs," thought Saunters, "is almost too heavenly a state of affairs for a sinner like me."

But Yulee after a little pause explained that Miss Morse was one of the winter boarders at St. Augustine, and that she knew everything, and was "so kind and so beautiful as ze queen of angels."

"Indeed," Saunters replied incredulously, "such immense erudition, goodness, and transcendent beauty are indeed a rare combination. Is Madame here a botanist too?" he asked, glancing at the unintellectual appearing woman who was clearing away the evening meal.

"Mozzer ees very wise in ze plants; she make them in most beautiful objects. Ze palmetto work of hats and of baskets they are all of her." And she explained in her soft patois, that they were gathering the young, yellowish white buds of the palmetto, and how necessary it was to cure the leaf before it expands and turns green, when it would be impossible to bleach it.

Saunters had always looked upon the fancy palm-work as so much useless trumpery, but now he found himself deeply interested in knowing that the buds of the cabbage palmetto make the best hats, but that there are few of these near St. Augustine, and most of the work is made of the Sabal serrulata, or saw-palmetto.

Yulee had several times spoken of her gypsy-like companion as mother, but Saunters could not believe that they were related. He fell into a second mistake, even worse than that of supposing her too unintellectual to study botany. To Saunters there were only two classes, — the illiterate plebeian, and "our set." Yulee's appearance would hardly assert her a member of this exclusive body; but he fell to wondering how she would look in another style of costume, and he felt that the result would be satisfactory. As to this woman whom Yulee called mother, she might be an octoroon nurse who had brought her up. He had heard that in the South children addressed their nurses as mauma or mammy. Still, the face was not quite African in its

ORIENTAL PALM.

suggestions; perhaps she was Spanish, or Indian, or Creole. Whatever she was, he dismissed her from his mind as totally common and uninteresting.

He felt that he had been silent rather longer than was quite polite, and rousing from his reverie asked, "What is it that you say you make from this palmetto?"

"Ze hats and basket, ze napkin-ring, ze brush to cause ze flies to depart, and ze — what you call zat sing — zat sing what go wibble-de-wobbledy, backward and forward, to make more cooler ze breeze?"

"You mean fans?"

"Oh yes, ze fans."

"You don't mean to say that the palmetto hats, which are all the style here, and which are so cool and light, are the kind you make?"

"To be course."

"Ah, you make them for yourself, I understand, merely for your own amusement. My sister has a mania for fancy-work, too; cuts birds and things out of cretonne and sews them on satin; fitted up my room for me, — little devils in black velvet, appliqué on Turkish towelling."

"But no, it is not so amusing; we have one leetle shop; it is so we do make our living."

"Oh!"

There was a pause during which Yulee worked industriously with her botanical specimens. They were arranged to her satisfaction at last, and she began to pick the palmetto buds to pieces.

"Would you like to see how we make ze plaits?" she asked.

"If you please; but would you mind telling me what you mean by plaits? I do not think I exactly understand." Nor did the hypocritical fellow at all care; but although he saw the moon rising over the pines, and knew that it was nearly time for him to withdraw and prepare his own camp at a little distance, he wished to prolong the interview as late as possible, and by deft questions hindered Yulee so effectually that she was a full half-hour in telling him how the palmetto had to be stripped at the divisions of the leaf, but not separated entirely from the stem, how it was then bleached for several nights, and after that cut into fine strands by a curious little affair which she showed him, — a small piece of wood, perhaps an inch in length, into which were set at regular intervals a number of needle points. She drew a strip of palmetto across this instrument, and it was torn into narrow, smooth ribbons, which she proceeded to plait for him into a fancy braid of eight strands. They did not always use so many, she admitted; and then he was curious to see all the different patterns which could be woven, and was interested in knowing that most of the plaiting was done by little girls, and that her mother sewed and shaped the hats after the plaits were formed, buying it by the yard from the children. He wished to order a hat for himself, he said, and decided, after some further conversation, to have it dyed black with pomegranate juice. He tried hard to continue the conversation by asking if she could not attach a veil to it in the English tourist style, so that he could wear it when gunning in mosquito districts; but Yulee was growing distraught and restless. At length she addressed a few words to her father in a strange musical language which reminded Saunters vaguely of Italian, and the man gave a shrill whistle.

An odd figure now limped into view from behind a cluster of scrub-palmetto. He was a specimen of the poor white of the South, but with something of Yankee shrewdness in his small bright eyes. His beard bristled over his gaunt sallow face, and his clothes in their tatters and general unkempt appearance betrayed long familiarity with jungle camp-life.

"Zees is our guide, Meester Alligator Joe," said Yulee, with the air of introducing a distinguished guest.

"Howdy, Mister?" said Joe.

"My name is Saunters," the young man explained, realizing for the first time that he had not introduced himself, — "Captain Clarence Saunters, of the Army."

"Wall, Cap'n, it's a-gettin' kinder late; an' ef you'd like to turn in, maybe you'll share our camp-fire over yonder."

"You will find Meester Alligator Joe one charming teller of story," said Yulee, engagingly.

Saunters protested that there was nothing he enjoyed so much as a hunter's or soldier's yarns told by a camp-fire; but he said it with very little enthusiasm, and took a lingering farewell of his hostesses, the elder woman lending him a blanket, which he found very acceptable. Yulee had disappeared within the tiny tent before he followed Mr. Ponce and Joe to the masculine side of the camp in the pine forest. Joe explained that his occupation was that of an alligator hunter. "I unites two perfeshuns, sir, — I'm a 'gator dentist and a nuss; I may say a wet-nuss, sir, for it's mighty sloppy business. I keeps a foundlin' hospital for little 'gator babies, and I shoots the old ones and relieves 'em of their teeth. I most generally carries two portmanteaus, — one for little alligators, and one for teeth and skins. I tans their hides likewise, and drives a right smart business with the Jacksonville shops. They all knows 'Alligator Joe,' though most people don't call me by my perfeshunal names; they knows me best as 'The Critter.' It's a sort of pet name that folks that I've guided about Floridy have give me. They say there never was such a critter as I am for finding his way through the lonesomest kind of swamp, or the biggest tangle of bresh that tuckered out one of yer college-bred

"THE CRITTER."

THE CAMP IN THE FOREST.

surveyors. When I'm on a pleasure tramp, I'm 'The Critter,' sir; when I'm on business, I'm 'Alligator Joe.'"

While "The Critter" was talking, he was deftly making Saunters a bed of Spanish moss, on which he now placed a large black valise as bolster.

"See here, my friend," exclaimed Saunters, observing this object suspiciously, "is that the valise you carry your alligator orphans in, or is it the dental collection? Because, if it's the teeth, they might be a trifle hard, and the little alligators would be perhaps — oh, well, we'll say squirmy."

"The Critter" assured him that he was not now on one of his professional tramps, and that the valise contained only his personal wardrobe; but in spite of this explanation, Saunters surreptitiously removed the valise before retiring. He wrapped the blanket about him, piled more fuel upon the fire, threw himself down beside it, and thought how odd and strange it all was. With all his affectations he had a kindly heart, and was not utterly and inanely vapid. His first glimpse of Yulee had touched his artistic nature; there was something in the present surroundings that appealed to the romantic. He remembered Borrow's description of the gypsy camp in the dingle, his picturesque meeting and sad parting with Isabel Berners, and all the wild charm of a roving life depicted so well in that strange book, "The Rommany Rye." For the instant Bohemia laid her charm upon his soul, and he fancied that it might be an agreeable thing to cut civilization and wander for the rest of his life through the Florida everglades; and so musing, hardly listening to "The Critter's" wonderful stories of alligator hunts and encounters, he fell asleep, and dreamed incoherently of driving a four-in-hand of alligators, with Yulee at his side, and the fat old creole or octoroon or gypsy, in footman's costume, at the back of the coach.

Morning came, and he parted from his new acquaintances, receiving directions from "The Critter" which could not fail to pilot him to

St. Augustine,—directions which it would have been well for him had he followed at once. But, attracted by Raphael Ponce's story of a creek which swarmed with duck, he plunged a little deeper into the pine woods, and enjoyed a morning of successful hunting, taking especial pains this time not to lose his way. His game, when shot, frequently fell into the creek, to be brought back by his faithful dogs. At last, a duck falling farther out than the rest, Turf launched boldly after it. Suddenly he let it fall, uttered a prolonged howl, and sank gradually into the water. Saunters comprehended at once that one of the alligators of which "The Critter" had told him so many seemingly impossible yarns, had seized his pet; he fired his gun, shouted, and threw sticks into the water without effect. The dog sank out of sight, and the troubled water became calm. It was only then that he noticed the singular conduct of the other dog, Field, who would ordinarily have swum for the sticks which Saunters threw into the water, but now crouched at his side howling with fear.

Saunters was filled with grief, and determined to return to the camp for "The Critter," to obtain his help in securing the body of his pet from the cruel teeth of its murderer. It was only an hour past noon when he regained the site of the camp; but the tent and the tip-cart were gone, and the ashes of the camp-fire with the remnants of the breakfast were the only traces which remained of his friends. It was impossible to guess in which direction they had gone, for the pine woods were crossed by a number of obscure wagon-tracks; and sadly and wearily he made his way to the nearest settlement, and from thence to St. Augustine. There he spent much of his time for days thereafter in visits to the different curiosity-shops, making vague inquiries with reference to dried grasses, Occola plumes, and palm work, in the hope of rediscovering the little Martyr of the Palm Branch.

Each time that he went it happened that he met a stately girl who was also looking for Miss Ponce. He noticed her at first only

DEATH OF TURK.

as having a more intelligent face than the ordinary girl of the period; but as he saw her day after day lingering before Yulee's window, he said to himself that she was, like the rest, inordinately fond of shopping and of filling her home with all manner of decorative trash.

CHAPTER IV.

HUMAN NATURE.

ON the afternoon of the day following the arrival of our party in Florida, Dr. Pettyman presented himself at the hotel, with several histories under his arm and his pockets bulging with manuscript. Being duly presented to Aunt Pen by Uncle Jonah and to Mrs. Morse by Madeleine, he joined the group upon the piazza, and began a dissertation upon Ponce de Leon, who made his first visit to Florida in 1512, seeking the Fountain of Youth, and who named the country from his landing on " Pascua Florida," or Easter Sunday.

He read of De Soto's visit, and of Jean Ribaut and René de Laudonnière, who came with the ill-fated French Huguenots in 1562 and 1564.

He spoke, in an easy manner and a pleasant tone of voice, of the terrible butchery of the French settlers under Laudonnière, by their Spanish neighbors, led by the tiger Menendez. Madeleine forgot to fan herself, and leaned forward with a look of horrified interest on her expressive face, as the Doctor, warming to his description, read : —

"Meantime poor Jean Ribaut's vessels are wrecked, a little below Matanzas Inlet; but his men get ashore, — some two hundred and fifty in one party, and the balance, three hundred and fifty, in another. Menendez informs them that if they will come over he will 'do to them as the grace of God shall direct.'"

HUMAN NATURE.

The Doctor continued the story, telling how Divine love, as understood by Menendez, directed that they should all be murdered on their march to St. Augustine as prisoners.

Cleopatra could not help confessing that he read very well; but she was certain that he did not feel what he read, — that he did not care in the least for the poor Huguenots butchered, "no por Franceses, sino por Luteranos" (not because they were Frenchmen, but because

ON THE VERANDA.

they were Lutherans), — and it irritated her that his reading should produce such an effect upon Madeleine. She was angry with his smooth oily accents, with the unctuousness with which he dwelt upon the horror, with the half-smile which quivered about his lips as he glanced at Madeleine's rapt face; and Cleopatra yawned impolitely as he completed his most telling period, — the revenge of the French Captain de Gourgues, who hung a number of Menendez' men, with the inscription, "Not because they were Spaniards, not because they were castaways, but because they were traitors, thieves, and murderers."

Madeleine looked up with a reproving glance, and Patrick burst into a merry laugh. "I did not mean to be so impolite," she said. "Dr. Pettyman is a fine elocutionist; he reminds me of the man who could repeat the word 'Nebuchadnezzar' with such pathos that it would bring tears to the eyes of all who listened. I am a little tired of those long-ago-dead Huguenots, however, and find it rather hard to squeeze out a tear in their memory. The St. Augustine of to-day is so peaceful and lazy, it does not seem as if any one could have energy enough here to butcher and massacre and do all those dreadful things. It is just the place to be sleepily mirthful, and to bask in the sun and read novels."

"Only, there are few novels worth reading," said Madeleine. "Oh, Patrick, *did* we bring 'Sir Galahad'?"

"Who is Sir Galahad?" asked Dr. Pettyman.

"It is one of the few modern novels worth reading," Madeleine replied enthusiastically. "I remember now I put it in mother's room. I wanted her to read it;" and Madeleine stepped through the long window into the cool chamber where Mrs. Morse was reclining on a lounge. She knelt by her mother's side, and in her sweet solicitude for her comfort forgot for a moment the errand on which she had entered.

"Who is the author of this remarkable novel?" Dr. Pettyman asked of Cleopatra.

"I don't know — that is, it is an anonymous work," she replied falteringly. "It is not a wonderful work of genius. Madeleine likes it because the hero expresses sentiments similar to her own. You would think him very silly, Dr. Pettyman, but I have heard Madeleine say that the only man whom she could endure was this hero on paper."

Dr. Pettyman seemed deeply interested; and when Madeleine returned with the book he looked it over carefully, reading some of the marked passages more than once. Madeleine showed him her favorite portions, and praised the book so extravagantly that strangers edged a little nearer and listened while Dr. Pettyman read extracts.

ENTRANCE TO THE OLD FORT

"Some way, it sounds just like you, Niece Madeleine," said Uncle Jonah.

"That's what I have always said," Madeleine replied excitedly. "Whoever wrote that book thinks just as I do about a great many topics. I wish I could meet the author. I know I should enjoy talking with him."

Cleopatra looked very much amused, and pulled down the light veil which she wore, though the sun was not shining in her eyes.

The Doctor deliberately wiped his eyeglass, and asked, "Is not the authorship of this book suspected in cultivated circles?"

"No," replied Madeleine; "the critics say it is some one hitherto unknown; and when I wrote to the publishers about it, they replied that the author was very particular that the secret should not be disclosed."

"Not to the world at large, possibly," said Dr. Pettyman; "but in the confidence of our friendly circle, I do not mind confessing, Miss Madeleine, that I wrote that book."

"You! impossible!" exclaimed Madeleine, looking as though a bomb had exploded at her feet.

Cleopatra started violently, and throwing back her veil regarded the Doctor with a stare which was positively tragic. "Do you mean to assert," she asked slowly, "that you, Dr. Pettyman, are the author of this book?"

"I am," replied the Doctor, putting on his glasses and smiling blandly. "A poor thing, perhaps; but such as it is, it is my own."

Cleopatra rose, and staggered into the house. She looked very pale, and the others believed that she felt ill. Madeleine was not surprised, when she knocked at her door a few moments later, saying, "Do come, Patrick; we are going to walk up to old Fort San Marco," to hear her reply faintly, —

"Please go away, dear; I have such a headache."

But Madeleine had no suspicion of what had occasioned Cleopatra's headache. She had wondered occasionally what the other secret could be which her friend had told her she found so hard to keep, but had not given the matter any serious thought, or had any suspicion that Cleopatra knew who had written "Sir Galahad," and why it was that the sentiments therein expressed tallied so precisely with Madeleine's.

And meantime Cleopatra lay on her bed, holding her throbbing temples within her hands. "I disliked him when I first saw him," she said to herself. "Shall I expose him at once, and show Madeleine that he is an impostor and a liar? No; he has some object in view, and I will let him go on and develop it a little further."

From that moment, though Dr. Pettyman little suspected it, he was studied by a watchful and suspicious pair of eyes, which weighed his words and actions in a balance heavily weighted by an act which he could never explain away or excuse.

At first Dr. Pettyman seemed to have made a great stride in Madeleine's regard by his stratagem. She no longer regarded him simply as an ethnologist, but as a man, and as a man with whom she was already well acquainted; for had he not given her of his best thought in his novel, and what were weeks of ordinary chit-chat, of teas and luncheons, of whist and German, to this?

Madeleine found it difficult to make up her party for San Marco. Cleopatra's headache prevented her from going; her mother was not equal to so long a walk; Aunt Pen was cross. "I promised Captain Saunters," she said, "that he should show us the fort."

"Then we'll go again, Aunt," replied Madeleine; "but we are not obliged to wait for him indefinitely."

This was the true cause of Aunt Pen's irritation. She had expected to see Captain Saunters appear at once and claim the privileges which she had extended to him, and she had just heard from him, through a politely expressed note, that he would be absent for some time, shooting in the pine barrens. It was not only a disappointment

to her plans, but, as it seemed to her, an insult; and here was this little nobody occupying the field with apparent success. No, she would not go to San Marco, — it was too hot; and Madeleine must not think of going there alone with Dr. What's-his-name, unless she wished people to think — Madeleine closed the door quickly, and Uncle Jonah good-naturedly consented to accompany them.

Dr. Pettyman and Madeleine walked side by side along the old sea-wall, engaged in close conversation. Dr. Pettyman had need of all his faculties to prevent his falling into the sea, or into some equally dangerous pitfall, in reference to " Sir Galahad," which Madeleine insisted on discussing: but he was wary, and they reached the castle moat without mishap, Uncle Jonah following, like an over-fed poodle, considerably in the rear. Then the Spanish coat-of-arms over the portal, the drawbridge, the scarp and counterscarp, and the old grass-grown barbican formed new topics of conversation. He launched boldly into the Seminole war, spoke of the sieges the old fort had sustained, and of the ambuscades laid by the Indians for the troops whenever they ventured to penetrate the swamps; and for the moment Dr. Pettyman was safe.

The old Castle San Marco, now called Fort Marion, has been used for some time as a prison for Indians. In this prison, presided over by Captain R. H. Pratt, was started some years ago the nucleus of Government training-schools for Indians, which have since proved so successful. The Captain was placed here in charge of a few Indians, some of them noted desperadoes, and all accused of crime. He treated them as men, and allowed some philanthropic ladies to teach them; and some of these prisoners, on their release, asked to be allowed to remain in the East and study more. They were sent to Hampton, which from that time was thrown open to the Indian as well as to the colored man. The Government, finding that the call for education on the part of the Indian was an increasing one, detailed Captain Pratt to open an Industrial School for Indians at Carlisle

Barracks, Pennsylvania. This school now stands at the head, not only of all Indian schools but of all schools, as an exponent of industrial training in the different trades.

Madeleine knew something of this history. She knew, too, that imprisoned at Fort Marion was the main part of Geronimo's band, the Apaches, whose capture had given the Government so much trouble, and she had hoped to have a view of the prisoners. She was much disappointed when told by the officer in charge that this was not permitted, as it had a bad effect upon the Indians to be looked upon as a show.

ONE OF GERONIMO'S BAND.

Dr. Pettyman assured her that they were very uninteresting creatures,— degraded to the last degree, and indescribably brutal and savage.

"Perhaps it is our fault," said Madeleine, "if this is so;" and at the same time a doubt as to the truth of the Doctor's assertion crept into her mind. "I wish I could have a good talk with Geronimo, and learn his side of the question."

"Geronimo and the other chiefs are at Fort Pickens," said the Doctor. "St. Augustine people wouldn't have him here. They were afraid of a general uprising, and a massacre, you know."

"How is this, Dr. Pettyman?" Madeleine asked suddenly, after a pause; "in 'Sir Galahad' you inveigh so gloriously against the inhumanity and injustice of our people to the Indians, and now you do not seem to believe in them at all."

Dr. Pettyman stammered an apology, and again turned the conversation to safer channels, explaining that the castle had been built by Indian labor under the Spaniards, and that captives had even been brought from Mexico to assist in quarrying the great blocks of coquina (a shell conglomerate) and in building the immense walls.

Sixty years they labored to complete it, before the globe and cross, with the inscription and the date 1756, were carved over the portcullis, with the castles of Castile and the rampant lions of Aragon. They strolled down the grassy moat to visit the city gate, — or rather the old

THE OLD GATE, ST. AUGUSTINE.

coquina gate-posts with their flanking fragments, which proved that the city was once a walled town, — and then back to the cathedral and plaza to search out other interesting reminders of old Spanish occupation.

CHAPTER V.

SWEET AND SOUR ORANGES.

BALMY days were threaded one after another like scented rosary beads upon a golden chain. Mrs. Morse grew stronger, and a delicate tint like that in the heart of a conch shell flushed her cheeks. She joined them in their walks and drives, and learned to love the old Spanish landmarks as well as the girls. Aunt Pen became reconciled to the recreancy of Captain Saunters by the appearance on the scene of a wealthy orange-planter Mr. Riel S. Tait, a middle-aged widower who took them all to see his plantation of oranges. The perfume of the blossoming grove was heavy on the air, and modern luxury had done all that wealth can do in the villa of the owner, which was presided over by his sister, a very fashionable woman. But to Madeleine this display and perfume were equally oppressive, and the rotund form of Mr. Tait bowling leisurely along the long promenades reminded her absurdly of the largest ball in a tenpin alley. "He looks like a prize orange dropped from one of his own trees," she whispered to Cleopatra. That young lady had just quartered an immense orange, and was proceeding to enjoy its luscious sweetness, when an expression of keen distress shot across her face.

"What is the matter, Pat?" cried Madeleine; "have you the toothache?"

"It's *sour!*" groaned Cleopatra. "Vinegar is nothing to it; it's concentrated lime-juice."

"I should have warned you," apologized Mr. Tait, who now approached. "Our native fruit is quite sour until grafted by the sweet variety, for which it makes an excellent stock."

"Then why don't you graft them all; and pray, why do you raise any sour oranges?" asked Cleopatra.

"Do you see that man sitting on the bench yonder under the live-oak? He is a manufacturer of champagne, and buys my sour oranges for that purpose."

MR. TAIT AND HIS GUESTS.

"I don't wonder he has such a sour expression," Madeleine remarked. "I have noticed him before, and was sure he was a misanthrope."

A dainty tea was served on the veranda of the cottage; and then Mr. Tait drove them home behind his dashing four-in-hand, the footman depositing at their door a hamper of oranges and a basket of orange blossoms.

But Madeleine placed the flowers outside her window. They sickened her; she was tired of society and junketing, and she opened her Moral Philosophy resolutely, and read far into the night.

In the morning she went, as she had gone every day for some time past, to see if Yulee Ponce had returned from her botanical excursion; and this time, as so often before, there was a well-made, well-dressed

THE SOUR ORANGE MAN.

back of the shop leading into a garden,— a tangle of bananas, clambering roses, palms, and blossoming flowers. An arched cloister or portico bordered the garden on two sides, giving it the semblance of a Spanish court, or patio. The floor of the portico was flagged with worn stones, and the pillars and arches were of gray coquina wreathed with clambering passion-vines and jasmine.

It was not make-believe theatrical Spanish architecture, like the two new hotels,— the Ponce de Leon with its bewildering miradors, loggia, wrought-iron balconies, gargoyles, gaudy tiles, and Moorish arches; or the Casa Monica, with its cavernous gateway, a restoration of the Puerta del Sol of Toledo. It was a veritable relic of Spanish occupation of the better class. Few such houses now remain, with their red roofs of corrugated tiles surmounting the quiet gray stone walls and flaring like a cactus blossom against the deep blue of the sky.

On a low chair in a shady angle Yulee sat braiding palmetto; while the stranger stood at a little distance, watching the operation with

OLD SPANISH HOUSE

interest. Yulee dropped her work and ran forward to meet Madeleine, taking both her hands and chattering like a parrot of the flowers she had found on her expedition. Suddenly she remembered that she had not introduced her guests, and did so in her stately Spanish manner. Then she darted into the house and brought out her herbarium and case of fresh specimens, and Saunters begged permission to remain and attend the botany lesson. He proved himself something of an adept as well, having given much attention to the subject. The morning sped away unconsciously, and the lesson might have been prolonged indefinitely had not Madame Ponce been seen laying the table for the midday meal. Captain Saunters accompanied Madeleine to her door, and told her as they walked how he had first met Yulee and how much she interested him. "I thank you," he said simply, "for what you are doing for her; you are opening a new existence to the girl."

CAPTAIN SAUNTERS CALLS.

After that it was but natural that they should meet frequently in the cool cloister at the back of the little shop. Sometimes Cleopatra came too, and joined in the readings or braided Yulee's plait while she pursued her studies. Cleopatra liked Yulee, but not with the enthusiastic fondness which Madeleine felt for her pupil. She liked Saunters also; there was something frank and open about him which had won her admiration from the first. He called often at the hotel; and Aunt Pen now approved of the lessons given to Yulee Ponce, which she had formerly regarded as a Quixotic missionary enterprise. She talked it all over with long-suffering Uncle Jonah; for in some way Mrs. Morse, though sisterly, and accessible on other topics, never liked to talk over her daughter's possible prospects. Mr. Tait had fallen in Aunt Pen's good graces because — a rather absurd reason, at first sight, — because it was so difficult to eat oranges nicely!

He had served oranges at his villa, he had sent them oranges since in hampers and baskets; but Aunt Pen could never divide one of the golden balls without making a mess of it. She had stained her heliotrope satin at the tea-party. She had wiped her dripping fingers on her best embroidered handkerchief when practising in private, and was aware that she had frequently made a spectacle of herself at the hotel table. If Madeleine should settle in Florida, Aunt Pen knew that it would be incumbent upon her to visit her niece and to eat of her nephew's oranges; therefore Aunt Pen turned her favor from Mr. Tait. Hearts have broken for less cause; but Madeleine was happily unconscious of the schemes with which her aunt amused herself during the interval between the meals, which were to her the chief events of the day.

Of course it not unfrequently transpired that Dr. Pettyman was reading to the ladies when Saunters came in with magnolias or mistletoe, water-lilies or tropical fruit. Sometimes the history was suddenly dropped to admire a curlew's rosy breast or a flamingo's scarlet wing; and the Doctor glared the rage he dared not speak, while the Captain told them of his hunting expeditions, of reedy creeks and yachting trips along the coast where the yacht was anchored among flocks of flamingoes. He invested the old fort with a new interest, and procured a special permit by which they were allowed to visit the interior. He explained Vauban's system of castle-building more clearly than the Doctor had done, showed the bastions, and took them up to the little pepper-pot watch-towers in which some Indians were crouching.

"It has all the background for a weird romance," said Cleopatra. "Only give us a night effect, a tangle of vines about the masonry,

and those figures might be ghouls or ghosts or bandits, as you choose. I presume thrilling dramas have really been acted here in the past."

"The present is dramatic enough for me," said the Captain, as he led them through the narrow passage-way between the tents with which the ramparts were crowded. "Here are four hundred and forty-

FLAMINGOES.

seven Indian prisoners, only ninety of whom are men, and possibly only half of those guilty of any outrage, the remainder torn from their homes by an act as arbitrary as the removal of the Acadians from Grand Pré. Good may come of it; but it is strange justice all the same, and will probably furnish material for a poem like that of 'Evangeline' to some writer of the twentieth century."

He introduced them to Chief Chatto, imprisoned he thought for no sufficient reason; and to Kieta and Martinez, Apache scouts, who had brought about in great part the surrender of Geronimo, and had been rewarded by imprisonment with the brigands. "Our Government does not discriminate over-nicely," he said rather bitterly.

They visited the school for the prisoners, carried on by those noble women, Miss Mather, Mrs. Caruthers, and the Misses Clark.

Madeleine looked on with keenest interest. "How quickly they learn," she said, "and what a noble cause to which to devote one's life!"

"Yes," replied the Captain; "Indians are interesting whether as foes or wards. I would rather be engaged in an actual Western campaign at this moment than idling in this American Italy."

Madeleine glanced at him with a gleam of admiration. "You are not over-complimentary," she said, "but I can understand the feeling. If I were a man I would want to *do* something."

Cleopatra laughed. "Just as if you were not doing something as a girl!" she said. "Captain Saunters, she has studied like a Trojan ever since we have been here, and has found time to coach Yulee Ponce every day."

The young man's expression softened. "I am glad you have taken up Yulee," he said. "What do you think of her, Miss Morse? Is she capable of education?"

"Indeed she is," replied Madeleine; "and she has a rather remarkable education already, though in irregular lines. I want her to go to Vassar for a special course in Science, but her family are so very poor. I could help her out of my own allowance, but could not quite afford to pay her entire tuition."

"Will you not let me share in this good work?" asked the young man. "I am deeply interested in this."

"Thank you, Captain, but I fear that Miss Ponce is too proud to accept such a gift at your hands."

"I am afraid she is. Will you not then allow me to do it in your name?"

"No, indeed, Captain Saunters; if Yulee would accept it from me, — and of this I am doubtful, — her gratitude would shame me so that I could not keep the secret."

"We might do this," suggested Cleopatra: "tell her that some benevolent man had founded a scholarship, — that's what Captain Saunters' offer amounts to, — and that you, Madeleine, have sent in her name as one of the competitors. Make her understand that it is a matter of passing the best examination or something of the kind. I think if we explain it all to Professor Hartley when we return to the college, he will aid and abet us by writing her an official letter stating her admission."

"How clever you are, Cleo!" said Madeleine, admiringly. "I am willing to enter into such a scheme;" and so it was arranged.

A bond of union seemed suddenly to have united Madeleine and the Captain. The young girl's quick intuition told her that he was interested, even more deeply than he professed to be, in Yulee, and was therefore not likely to be "ridiculous" with her. She could chat with him familiarly now without any fear of being misunderstood, or of encouraging undesired affection. There was not the least spark of coquettishness in the girl's grand nature, and she was honestly thankful that Saunters did not care for her, except in this frank brotherly way, which was so pleasant.

As for Saunters, the masculine heart is so complex that it would be hard to analyze it at this juncture. He admired Yulee, — her beauty, her bewitching ways, fascinated him, — but he had not told her in set terms of this admiration. A certain caution, peculiar to his class, told him to wait and see what effect cultivation would have upon this wild flower. Meantime he genuinely liked Madeleine, and it was very pleasant to bask in her society.

"You must not study too hard," he said, with kindly concern as they strolled homeward along the sea-wall. "This climate is not favorable to intellectual effort. You must take care of your health."

"That is what I say," chimed in Cleopatra. "Madeleine has grown quite pale since we came here. Aunt Pen threatens to take us all away. She thinks there is malaria about the hotel, and is of the opinion that it would do us good to go with her husband when he makes his trip up the Ocklawaha."

"Oh, no!" exclaimed Madeleine; "I would not be able then to assist Yulee, and she is progressing so nicely."

"Is there no way of combining study with exercise?" mused Saunters. "A dashing gallop would bring the blood into your cheeks;" then, as Madeleine shook her head, he added: "I have it; I will take you all for a yachting trip to Matanzas or Anastasia Island. The studies could go on as usual, and it will do your mother good."

Madeleine hesitated. "Yulee and I have talked of making such an expedition for sea-weed," she said. "I am afraid, however, that mother is not strong enough yet, and I could not leave her."

Contrary to expectation, Mrs. Morse thought the trip would benefit her; and, the next morning being sure to be cloudless, a party was hastily made up for Anastasia Island, including our tourists, Yulee Ponce, and Dr. Pettyman. The Doctor, however, could not be found, and his place was filled by Mr. Tait. Aunt Pen, too, who had been very enthusiastic up to the last moment, dropped out as they were starting, saying — which was true — that she was a very poor sailer. The others started in high glee. Saunters had found, to his disgust, that none of the yachts were available at such short notice, and had been obliged to content himself with a fruit-schooner, just in with a cargo of sponges from the Bahamas. As they started, Cleopatra opened a locker that Captain Saunters had indicated as a good place in which to store wraps, and found it filled with oranges. She threw two of them into the air, catching them like a juggler.

"Ugh! said Aunt Pen, shrugging her shoulders as she turned away; "I wonder Floridians don't turn into oranges."

"Sweet or sour, which will you choose?" laughed Cleopatra.

"Unfortunately, we cannot tell from the outside appearance," said Madeleine.

"Almost as bad as choosing a partner for life," remarked Uncle Jonah, jocosely; "the handsomest ones are pretty sure to be the sourest."

CHAPTER VI.

THE CAPTAIN'S WAGER AND THE DOCTOR'S REVENGE.

WHAT a trip it was! They did not put boldly to sea, but loitered down the Matanzas River, which is here a salt-water estuary, with Anastasia Island forming a natural breakwater on the east. They started a flock of pelicans in a reedy bayou, and "The Critter," whom Captain Saunters had engaged to help in the management of the boat, told them a yarn of the pelicans he had seen at the mouth of the St. John, — "that tame that you couldn't skeer 'em, an' all so took up with squabbling over their fishing that I done waded out and bagged three on 'em by ketching 'em by the legs."

The Captain produced fishing-tackle, and all settled themselves to fishing. The water swarmed with salt-water trout, mullet, whiting, red snapper, and other fish.

Cleopatra was so fortunate as to catch a pompano. "What a curious name!" she said. "Was it Pompey or Madame de Pompadour who was fond of them?"

"I cannot say," replied the Captain; "I only know that it is a most toothsome fish, the aristocrat of these Southern waters."

They had made their way along the Matanzas without sails, assisted only by the current; but after a few hours they spread canvas, and returning nearly to St. Augustine stood out for Anastasia Light.

PELICANS FISHING.

The breeze was fresh, and the water broken; but no one was ill, and their shaking up only gave them a sense of exhilaration and a keen appetite. They crossed a school of porpoises playing clumsily at leap-frog. Suddenly every black fin disappeared.

"We have frightened them away," said Madeleine; "no, there is a white one close to the boat."

"A white porpoise? Impossible!" replied Saunters.

"But I am quite sure," Madeleine insisted. "It was very near. I dropped it a biscuit which it snatched greedily from my hand. There it is now!"

All looked in the direction in which she pointed, and Saunters uttered a cry, while "The Critter" exclaimed: "A shark, sure as guns! Well, you is lucky that he didn't take your hand along with the biscuit."

Captain Saunters improved the occasion to examine the fair hand closely, but finding it unscathed, was obliged very reluctantly to relinquish it. "It was the shark, and not our boat, which frightened the porpoises," he said.

"THE CRITTER" SPINS A YARN

A few moments later the boat's keel grated on the sand of Anastasia Island, and a picnic dinner, for which their cruise had given them a keen appetite, was prepared and despatched.

Mr. Tait's negro cook Elisha, who proved invaluable in preparing the dinner, seeing some snipe fly by, shouldered a shot-gun and was soon out of sight. He returned late in the afternoon with a string of birds and a marvellous story of how he had found them in a neighboring marsh engaged in combat with some bull-frogs. He produced a banjo of one string from the boat, and began, in true negro style, to improvise a ballad descriptive of his adventures. This was a favorite amusement of Elisha's; there was hardly an experience or adventure which he would not turn into rhyme, and Mr. Tait had brought him anticipating that he might be seized by one of his poetical spasms.

"Said de bull-frog to de snipe,
  'Oh, come an' dine wid me;
I'se jellies an' ices an' strawberries ripe,
  An' plenty of water fo' tea.'

"Says de sandpiper to de frog,
  'Yo' voice am mighty harsh;
Yo'se ketched a cold settin' on dat log ;
  I don' cah to dine in a marsh.'

"Says de bull-frog to de snipe,
  'Yo' airs done make me sick.'
So de snipe held his claw fo' a friendly gripe
  An' de frog he swallowed him quick.

"Now de moral ob dese jokes, —
  An' here my story ends, —
Is dat spiteful, 'ceitful, low-down folks
  Doan make de bess kine ob friends."

"I will take warning by your story," said Madeleine, "not to be too intimate with unworthy people."

"I wish she would," thought Cleo; "but if a certain wicked frog I know of has any designs on my bird, I think I know how to circumvent them."

Yulee and Madeleine now separated from the party to seek and find the choicest sea-weed in little pools left in the hollows by the retreating tide.

"Here is a bit of Sargassum!" Yulee exclaimed. "I wonder

whezzer it has been washed in from Sargazo Sea, in which you did tell me Columbus to be tangle on his way to zis country."

Madeleine examined the strange plant, which forms a floating flower-bed by means of countless little life-preservers or fruit-like bladders, — sea-grapes, the Neapolitans call them.

THE FROG AND THE SNIPE.

"They look like mistletoe," said Cleopatra, winding a spray about a pickle-jar. "What a lovely decorative scheme for a vase!"

"It is marvellous how many exquisite shapes they take," said Madeleine, enthusiastically. "I have seen a sea-weed, the Dasya elegans, that resembled chenille, and other varieties that were like skeins of silk, waving plumes, ferns, coral, fungi, and all the capricious shapes of frost. I remember a poem which struck my fancy on this subject: —

> 'Was this the fringe of a sea-nymph's robe,
> Caught in the door of a coral cave,
> Loosened by waters that span the globe
> And tossed ashore on a foamy wave?
>
> 'Was that the tip of a dancing plume
> That decked the head of a mermaid queen?
> Or refuse threads from an elfin loom
> Matching her mantle of pale sea-green?
>
> 'Were these the trees of a mimic isle,
> Never at loss for the sun or dew?
> Or only the branches that decked awhile
> A fairy boat with its fairy crew?
>
> 'O little mosses, perfect and fair,
> Emerald crimson and brown and jet,
> Fashioned with infinite skill and care,
> The charm of the sea is with you yet.'"

"That poem was evidently written by a woman," said Captain Saunters, who had followed them. "To a man the sea-weed brings thoughts of long voyages and foreign places. They come —

> 'From Bermuda's reef; from edges
> Of sunken ledges
> In some far-off bright Azore:
> From Bahama, and the dashing
> Silver-flashing
> Surges of San Salvador.
>
> 'From the tumbling surf that buries
> The Orkneyan skerries,
> Answering the hoarse Hebrides:
> And from wrecks of ships and drifting
> Spars, uplifting
> On the desolate rainy seas.'"

Madeleine gave him a little glance of surprise. He had thought of the poetic phase suggested by these lower forms of creation, which few notice or care for. They strolled along the beach, Yulee returning with the sea-weed to the boat; and the conversation took a more serious turn, passing from poetry into deeper channels.

"How beautiful it all is!" said Madeleine; "I had no idea that America was so fascinating."

"You should see the West," replied Saunters. "I am fretting to be back on the prairies; better a life of hardship and danger worthy of a man than falling to pieces in idleness!"

"The more I think of it," said Madeleine, "the more I am impressed by the fields which this great new country offers for enterprise and endeavor. There is so much to be done for humanity. There is the labor question in the East, the negroes here in the South, and the Indians in the West, and people nearer us still, friends and sisters like Yulee, who need our help, — mental and heart help, I mean. But — pardon me, Captain Saunters, if I offend — I can hardly see the need for the sword in our age, and I would like to know your reason for belonging to the army."

"I joined it from pure love of adventure," he replied frankly; "but I have studied the matter seriously since, and believe that until the Indian problem is settled we must be able to coerce as well as to educate and reform. The labor question, which you have touched upon, may yet demand armed force for the protection of law. Then again I, for one, do not see myself called upon to beat my sword into a pruning-hook so long as such a traitorous and disgraceful community as the Mormons bids defiance to the authority of the United States."

"I hope all these questions will be settled without war," said Madeleine, gravely; "but there is certainly much for the wisest to think of, and much which the weakest can do. The great question for each of us is to ascertain just how and where we can best serve our age. There is one grand hymn which acts on my spirit like a trumpet call; it urges us all to make fair and costly bequests to the future, and invokes aid in these words: —

> 'By each saving word unspoken,
> By thy truth as yet half won,
> By each idol yet unbroken,
> By thy will yet poorly done,
> Hear us, hear us,
> Thou Almighty! help us on.'"

There was a deep, sweet reverence as well as earnestness in the girl's tone. They were silent a moment, and then Saunters said, "How different you are from other girls!"

Her whole manner changed instantly. "Do you know that is not at all a pretty speech?" she said archly. "If you mean that other girls are not nice, I will never admit it in the world; and if you mean that I am not, I shall not like it any better."

"Oh! all girls are nice," said the young man, gallantly. "I have known half a dozen who were like you in some one particular, but none who united all your characteristics. There is my cousin Kitty, — she is jolly and pretty, but that's all there is of her; and my sister Mary is good, and talks as intelligently as any man about these questions which you and I have been discussing. You ought to know my sister Mary; you would like her, and perhaps she would learn from you to combine her austere virtues with more attractive graces. Then there is Mrs. General Dasher. She's uncommonly clever in another way; quotes poetry and writes it too, and plays the banjo like an angel. You remind me of her in certain ways, but some way as if you were the whole batch of them rolled into one, with a distinctive something of your own thrown in."

The conversation was becoming more personal than Madeleine liked, and she adroitly drew it into other channels.

When they returned to the boat they found Mr. Tait and Uncle Jonah engaged in earnest conversation. They drew Captain Saunters aside, and Mr. Tait asked if he was quite certain as to the sanitary condition of their schooner. "I have been rummaging in the hold," he said, "and I don't like an odor of fermentation which I find there.

I fear she has been imperfectly cleaned since her return from the West Indies."

"Her cargo was sponges," replied Saunters; "I thought they were a clean nice freight."

"Yes, we have found a few," replied Uncle Jonah, "and they look very nice. I guess it is all right."

While they were speaking, Madeleine was already examining them; and connected with one very fine and soft, of the variety used by surgeons, she discovered a pretty piece of violet fan coral. "Can I have it for my collection?" she asked; and no objection occurring to those who stood near, the coral was placed with her sea-weed, and the sponge in her toilet-case.

"AS THEY DRIFTED BACK BY SUNSET."

Only an inoffensive-looking bit of sponge; but such things have been as full of deadly mischief as many a smooth-spoken soft human tongue!

As they drifted back to St. Augustine by sunset and moonlight, Uncle Jonah spoke of his projected trip up the Ocklawaha. "Let us make it as a party," he suggested, "and after that trip take a steamer up the St. John's to Titusville, and then a yacht trip like this of to-day along the Indian River."

Mrs. Morse professed herself not at all tired, and approved of the plan; but Madeleine said that St. Augustine was so delightful that she could not think of leaving it so soon.

"You should see Fernandina on your way north," said Saunters, "if only for the sake of Dungenesse; it is one of the Paradises of Florida."

"What is Dungenesse?" asked Cleo.

"It was the seat of General Nathanael Greene, granted him in return for his services during the War of the Revolution. It is on an island about eighteen miles long, just opposite the Georgia and Florida boundary. The stone house is now only a ruin; but the whole estate is a riot of brilliant roses, magnolias, camellias, azaleas, and tropical fruits and flowers. It is a natural labyrinth, a conservatory escaped from glass. You must certainly see it."

HER FAVORITE BOOK.

And still Madeleine insisted that she did not wish to go anywhere. St. Augustine was good enough; the two months which they had already spent here seemed only so many days.

"Most devoutly do I wish that you may long continue in this mind!" said the Captain.

"What a delightful experience it was!" said Madeleine, the next morning. "There is nothing worth picking up after it but dear old 'Sir Galahad;'" and taking her favorite book she ensconced herself in a rocker on the veranda. She had not read far when Dr. Pettyman was announced. A frown involuntarily crossed her forehead as she thought that she must lay down her book. The next instant she laughed at herself. "Why, here is the man," she thought, "who has written the book, and must have all these noble thoughts in his heart, and a great many others as well worth the hearing." And she greeted the little man with a pleasant smile, regretting that the other ladies had all gone over to the old nunnery to buy some of the Sisters' lace, and that Uncle Jonah was busy preparing for his journey.

But Dr. Pettyman did not pretend to regret their absence. He had long wanted just this little opportunity to destroy Madeleine's growing faith in the Captain. It was a delicate task, and he began very cautiously and subtly, insinuating vague charges against the Captain's character, — floating impressions which he said might not be true; and even if he were not a strictly honorable man it was no one's business to tear the mask aside so long as he did no positive harm.

Madeleine's pupils distended as he maundered on, and at last when she could bear it no longer she cried: "Dr. Pettyman, this is unfair; say what you mean. Captain Saunters is our friend; if he is unworthy of our confidence, we ought to know it. Tell us definitely what you know against him."

Dr. Pettyman appeared greatly embarrassed. "Captain Saunters is a great favorite with your aunt," he said. "I am doubtful whether it was from her or from him that I understood that you also were greatly predisposed in his favor, — that, if not actually engaged, still such an event might be anticipated."

"No one had any right to tell you that. It is not true, though it sounds a little like Aunt Pen at her wildest. Captain Saunters, I am positive, is too much of a gentleman to talk so lightly of any lady of his acquaintance."

Dr. Pettyman assumed a look of deep commiseration. "Do you think so?" he asked doubtfully.

'I know so," the girl replied indignantly; "and, Dr. Pettyman, these vague innuendoes are not to your credit."

The Doctor straightened up with a well-simulated air of offended dignity. "It is possible that your estimate of Captain Saunters may not be overdrawn when he is at his best." he said; "but, my dear Miss Morse, when the wine is in and the wits are out, and one sits late at the club-house with a few jolly fellows, one becomes confidential and sometimes boastful. Much which I have to complain of in our friend I cannot repeat to you; but there is one circumstance which does concern you, and painful as it is for me to act in the matter, you perhaps ought to know. On your first arrival in Florida it was rumored that you were a young lady with a violent antipathy to the society of gentlemen, and Captain Saunters hearing this laid a high wager that you would accept his attentions, at least so far as to take a yachting trip with him. I am sorry to say that he has won the stakes."

A bright spot burned on each of Madeleine's cheeks. "You say that Captain Saunters bet a sum of money about my susceptibility to his attractions — just as a sporting-man might bet on a horse — in the public club-house! I don't believe it!"

Dr. Pettyman rose, bowed, and took his hat. Madeleine did not attempt to detain him. Seeing that his injured manner did not impress her, he wheeled and remarked: "Since my word is called in question, may I ask you, Miss Morse, to inquire of Captain Saunters whether he did or did not make such a bet! Perhaps you will believe him."

Cleopatra, having returned from the lace expedition, came out upon the veranda as the Doctor took his departure. "What is the matter, dear?" she asked as she noted Madeleine's excitement. Madeleine repeated what she had just heard.

"I don't believe it!" exclaimed Cleopatra.

"That is just what I said, but he told me to ask the Captain."

"Well, why don't you do so?"

"Never! I would not insult him by repeating such a story."

"It is a greater insult to let it lie and rankle in your mind when a word might clear it up. There he is, strolling this way. You *must* ask him."

"I can't; it is too humiliating."

"Then I will. Go into the house and leave it all to me. I shall know before he opens his mouth, by the very way he looks, whether it is true or not."

Madeleine vanished; and the Captain took a chair, inquiring after all the ladies.

"You shall see them presently," Cleopatra replied, "if you will kindly set my mind at rest on one point first."

The Captain smiled. "If it is in my power," he said.

CLEOPATRA AND THE CAPTAIN.

Cleopatra fidgeted with the feather fan, pulling out the pretty pink down in her abstraction. There did not seem to be any way to soften what she had to say or to make it agreeable, and she boldly seized the bull by the horns. "Captain Saunters, did you ever make a bet?"

He seemed amused by her repressed vehemence. "You will spoil that fan," he said. "No, I am not a betting man. I think I never made a regularly registered bet in my life."

Cleopatra did not look satisfied. "Can you assure me, Captain Saunters, that you never made a wager that you could induce Madeleine to go yachting with you?"

A sudden light burst upon the Captain; he became very grave. "My dear Miss Atchison," he said hesitatingly, "it was very thoughtless. I cannot express how deeply I have regretted this. It was before I had met Miss Morse— Will you not let me explain?"

Cleopatra had risen, her eyes flashing with indignation. "It is true, then!" she exclamied. "No, Captain Saunters, there can no explanation be made;" and she entered the hotel, leaving the discomfited Captain standing bewildered and wretched.

CHAPTER VII.

UP THE OCKLAWAHA.

PERHAPS it would have availed the Captain little if Cleopatra had allowed him the scanty grace of pleading his own cause. It is the pity of real life that very few heroes are consistently heroic; somewhere the true metal of the statue is mixed with miry clay, and the people we admire may have very sad faults.

Captain Saunters had been thoughtless and careless, but there was in him the making of better things. Madeleine had stirred his more earnest nature, and already he looked back at his old idle existence with scorn. He turned over the situation in his mind; and though it was not as bad as the girls understood it, he confessed to himself that it was quite unpardonable. He had been piqued, surprised, into the bet by the Doctor. It had not occurred in the club-house, as the Doctor had led them to infer, to the scandal and amusement of all St. Augustine, and he had repudiated the remark almost as soon as he had made it. Still, words let fall can never be really unsaid, and he could not deny them. "I will see her to-morrow," he said to himself, "and tell her the whole thing from beginning to end, and that I can't understand how I came to do such an ungentlemanly act. Perhaps, when she sees how really repentant I am, she will forgive me."

Meantime the girls were deeply hurt. "To think," said Madeleine, "that yesterday I actually thought him an honorable and delightful man, with even a more interesting and finer nature than the Doctor's, in spite of his charming book."

"Men are all horrid," replied Cleopatra. "I never want to see him again."

"We need not," replied Madeleine; "Uncle Jonah leaves tomorrow for the Ocklawaha, and he will be delighted when he learns that we have decided to go with him."

And so it came about that when the Captain, a little hopeful over the carefully framed explanation which he had thought out, called the next day, he was just in time to receive a parting handgrasp from Aunt Pen and a cool bow from the girls as the omnibus rolled away to the train. What exasperated him still more was the fact that he was sure that he saw Dr. Pettyman inside the omnibus, though his small sharp face was nearly eclipsed by Madeleine's great Gainsborough hat. He went at once to Yulee Ponce's little shop, and learned from her that Miss Morse intended to stop at St. Augustine on her return to the North, and had arranged a course of study for her to pursue in the mean time. This was encouraging so far as it went, and on this scrap of hope Saunters lived many days. Only the day after they left, his heart gave a wild throb as he saw a well-remembered hat among the promenaders on the seawall; but the next instant showed him that though the hat was really Madeleine's, the face beneath it was that of the hotel chambermaid to whom the girl had given a quantity of her cast-off finery.

Strange to say, his affection for Madeleine grew with the difficulties laid in its way. Yulee's beauty lost its attractiveness, and he found himself dwelling on Madeleine's ideas and aims, and shaping his own plans and conduct by them. We have heard of the lady to know whom was a liberal education. Saunters had found it still more to know Madeleine, for she had stimulated not only his mental but his moral nature. A poet has said, —

> "You love! That's high as you shall go;
> For 't is as true as Gospel text,
> Not noble then is never so,
> Either in this world or the next."

A WELL-REMEMBERED HAT.

Dr. Pettyman also loved Madeleine, or thought he did; but the affection awakened no craving after nobler being, only a low chuckling satisfaction as he sat beside her on the steamer deck sweeping up the noble St. John's in the glorious weather, — a base satisfaction with the neat way in which he had outwitted his rival.

They steamed up the St. John's to Palatka, passing orange plantations and winter hotels, swamps and jungles, evidences of man's enterprise and still unexplored jungles, almost side by side. Wild ducks flew overhead, and occasionally a dark mass lifted itself and disappeared, which some one asserted was an alligator.

"The Critter" was among a group of rough-looking men on the lower deck, telling his Munchausen stories. "Yes, sir," said he, "I was gunnin' on this very river in '58, an' I seen a floatin' island comin' down with the current. I rowed over nigh enough to see that though the island wa'n't very big, it was a perfect flower-garding, jis covered with blossoms an' posies. Wall, gentlemen, I was just about to step from my boat on to it when the hull sunk outer sight quicker than you could say Jack Robinson. You see it was a 'gator who had plated himself pretty well with mud, and seeds had blown on it and sprouted into the garding I tell ye of."

"The Critter's" story was received with laughter, which was rather approving than derisive. He was well known on the river, and no one tired of hearing his tales, particularly as he never repeated them in exactly the same way.

At Palatka our travellers were transferred from the great river-steamer to the narrow little craft in which they were to thread the tortuous channel of the Ocklawaha, which empties into the St. John's a few miles above, opposite the little town of Welaka.

They turned into "the mysterious river" late in the afternoon; for Uncle Jonah had planned that they should have the *night* trip, with all its glamour of torchlight reflections in the inky water. The stream was so narrow that the trees arched over on either side, forming a covered canal. The torch in the great iron crate over the pilot-house was filled with pitch-pine and lighted; the sparks danced and flickered away into the blackness, startling the herons asleep on one leg, and giving glimpses of cypress swamps or vistas up some tributary or everglade. Often the little river broadened into a pool or lake where the trees still grew knee-deep in the water or their twisted roots suggested an army of writhing snakes worthy the imagination of a Doré.

The little steamer was a stern-propeller, built especially for this river, with a wheel-house high up forward, a little deck aft, and four state-rooms between. Only Mrs. Morse and Aunt Pen tried these state-rooms until morning; the others sat through the night fascinated by the weird effects.

The Doctor did not fail to improve his opportunity. He saw that Madeleine was impressed by the strangeness of the scene, and he strove to connect himself with it by descanting volubly upon its beauties, and by drawing comparisons between this experience and moonlight nights

FLOATING ALLIGATOR ISLAND

in Venice. He shrewdly thought that if he could become so identified with this night that whenever it was recalled he would seem a part of the experience, he would have scored a considerable advantage.

The Doctor had another important circumstance in his favor. Madeleine, like nearly all college girls, placed an undue importance upon intellect and culture. She told herself that the mind was everything, and that mental graces were far to be preferred to bodily ones. She was punishing herself secretly for having been pleased by the Captain's prepossessing appearance, his manly carriage, his frank, boyish smile, and even his courage, which she told herself was purely physical. His education at West Point had indeed been more severe than the Doctor's college-skimming; but the Doctor quoted glibly from the classics, was an empyric in science, and a showy pretender in history. Madeleine had not discovered his shallowness, and was now conscientiously attempting to force herself to endure him. Cleopatra poked covert fun at his littleness, and quoted such lines as —

> "With his fine white teeth, and his cheek like a rose,
> And his neat cravat and his diamond pin,
> And the nice little mustache under his nose,
> And the dear little tuft on the tip of his chin."

But that was of no consequence. Madeleine analyzed laboriously the entire picture, and told herself that it was not derogatory to have fine teeth or a fresh complexion, or to dress carefully; and as to being small of stature, Isaac Watts was a little man, and so was many another giant of intellect. As to moral and heart qualities, she gave him the credit for possessing all that was so delightfully described in "Sir Galahad." She was angry with the Captain for assuming, as she believed, a seriousness which he did not feel, and leading her to speak of her most sacred aspirations, perhaps only to make her a jest at the club-house. With her resentment was mingled a suspicion that as she had overrated the Captain, so she had possibly underrated the Doctor.

She gave herself up now to the glamour of the night. It was the Doctor's good star that glanced on them through the rifts in the overhanging branches. Cleopatra brought out her guitar and played and sang Spanish serenades, — light, lilting love-songs, with ringing choruses, — " Teresita Mia," and college ditties such as are sung on moonlight nights by the students of Salamanca.

Cleo was chatting with Uncle Jonah at a little distance, and the Doctor said very softly in Madeleine's ear, " Why not drift on thus forever?" and Madeleine knew that he did not mean that they should spend the remainder of their lives in excursion trips up and down the Ocklawaha; and with the comprehension of what he did mean, came the swift conviction of how impossible it would be.

Before she could speak, Cleopatra drew her arm in hers, saying, " It is almost daybreak; we must have a little sleep."

She tried to realize what had happened, but was too weary; and she fell asleep almost as soon as her head touched the pillow.

When they awoke, late the following day, they found the boat moored in the quiet waters of Silver Spring. After breakfast they took row-boats, the better to understand the wonderful clearness and depth of this beautiful lake. Madeleine stepped into the skiff with her mother and Uncle Jonah. She was a little shy of the Doctor this morning, and not quite sure of what he had said or meant. Had she dreamed it? No; the Doctor was embarrassed and conscious also. How very insignificant he looked, helping Aunt Pen into the boat! But then Aunt Pen was really an enormous woman. Now he was offering to help Patrick, and he was only up to her shoulder. What an absurd couple they would make marching up the church aisle together! Preposterous! How differently things looked by daylight!

She turned resolutely to a contemplation of Nature about her. For sixty feet one could look straight down through the pellucid water to the bottom of the basin. Uncle Jonah dropped coins and

A CYPRESS SWAMP.

other small objects, and Madeleine held her mother while she watched them fluttering slowly to the pebbles which lined this great punchbowl. She was glad to notice how well her mother looked, and she clung to her tenderly even after she had ceased to lean over the edge of the boat.

All around the margin of the lake the tropical vegetation framed the lovely mirror, — oaks, cypresses, sweet-gums, willows, magnolias, and palms festooned with luxuriant vines, with mistletoe and the gray drapery of the Spanish moss.

"It makes me think of Druids' beards," said Madeleine.

"Or the tails of Bo-peep's sheep," said Cleopatra, mischievously.

"It makes excellent mattresses," said Uncle Jonah, prosaically. "They have a factory for preparing it for upholstery purposes at one of the river towns."

"There is another golden variety," said the Doctor, "called Woman's Hair."

They drifted about in their tiny skiffs, now floating lazily in a bed of lily-pads, now darting down a shadowy lagoon a little way into the jungle, startling some wild turkeys and themselves frightened by the plunge from the bank into the water of a huge turtle, which, as Cleopatra said, "might just as well have been an alligator."

"I wonder whether this magnificent wild conservatory will ever be drained and planted and staked out into miserable little town-lots," mused Madeleine.

"I hardly think there is any immediate danger," replied Cleopatra, dryly, "that the crowded city poor will steal away the homes of the dear lovely little alligators."

A FLORIDA TYPE.

Madeleine laughed. "But surely there is room for both in our wide country; and just to wander through such a natural park as this is a great privilege. How beautiful Silver Spring must have been before man ever found it; when it really belonged to the deer and the other shy creatures of the wood. Do you know I fancy this must have been the Fountain of Youth which Ponce de Leon heard of."

"That idea has been advanced," said the Doctor, "but I fear it can never be definitely proved."

At the steamer wharf Cleopatra found opportunity to use her camera, and obtained a number of new Florida types,—negroes busily lading the boat or lazily looking on, too well-to-do for active exertion. A benevolent-appearing man in a broad hat and light duster, who was to drive them across the country to an inland town, was greatly interested in the photography, and Cleopatra unstrapped her album for his inspection. He could not understand the instantaneous process, and certain views of persons and animals in motion puzzled him completely.

"TOO WELL-TO-DO FOR EXERTION."

"Used to take tin-types myself," he explained. "Never could keep folks still, specially babies."

He evidently thought the Doctor was guying him when he was informed that photographs were now taken in $\frac{1}{2600}$ part of a second.

"It does seem incredible," said Cleopatra; "but more wonderful things than this have been accomplished. You know there is a theory that the eye retains for a moment the image which is formed upon it by light. I remember reading a story of a murdered man's eye being photographed and the portrait of his murderer found within it. Well, that is quite possible; for I have heard recently that

SILVER SPRING IN FORMER TIMES.

a fly was killed in front of a cat, and one of its microscopic eyes photographed, and the image of the cat found within it."

The man in the duster hemmed softly. "Next thing that chap will photograph the eye of a needle," he said, "and tell us he has found the camel in it."

He had a peculiar dry chuckle, and his closely shaven face displayed a quantity of good-natured lines formed by continual smiling.

"I wonder what his business is," whispered Cleopatra. "Did you ever see a jollier countenance?"

As they piled into the spring-wagon and buckboard waiting for their transportation, Uncle Jonah asked if he was connected with the hotel to which they were going.

"Well, sorter," he replied; "leastways the hotel's connected with me. I own it and a good share of the balance of the town."

As they drove on, the wild character of the woods disappeared, and orange groves took their place.

THE SWEET-ORANGE MAN.

"That's my land," he remarked; "I've got it pretty well put down to oranges, and I ain't no fault to find with the crop this year."

"What a contrast he is to the Sour-Orange Man we saw at Mr. Tait's!" said Cleopatra in a low voice; and almost as if he had heard her their new friend continued,—

"Sweet oranges is the payingest crop there is. There's all the differ between oranges that there is 'twixt humans. I hain't no use for a sour orange or a sour-tempered man. They calls me the 'Sweet-Orange Man' about these parts; an' I dunno as it's meant so, but I takes it as a compliment. 'Vinegar never catches flies,' says I, an' a good-natured man generally catches all the luck that's going."

The Sweet-Orange Man's estimate of himself was not overdrawn. It was to buy land that Uncle Jonah had taken this trip; and before he left the region he had yielded to the wiles of the good-humored speculator, and had invested largely in orange plantations.

CHAPTER VIII.

A CAMP-MEETING AND A GREAT EMERGENCY.

THAT evening they attended a negro camp-meeting. What a weird sight it was, — a sea of dusky faces lighted by flaring torches, the impassioned words and gestures of Brother Cheer-the-mourners-Rouse-the-sinners Robinson, the gray-haired pastor, the groans and fervent amens from the congregation! They were singing, as the visitors took their places, a strange wailing song, swelling and falling like the wind in a pine forest, —

> "Did you eber hear the hammers ring
> As dey nailed our Sabeyer down,
>   Chilleren?
> Dey nailed our Sabeyer down;
>   He died fo' you, an' he died fo' me,
>   An' he died fo' us all on Calvary,
>   Chilleren!
>   He died fo' de whole roun' worl'
>
> "Did n' you promise de Lord to take care ob de lambs,
> An' bring 'em at de welcome day to his han's,
>   Chilleren,
> Who died fo' de whole roun' worl'?
> He died fo' you," etc.

And now the old pastor rose and announced his text, "By dere fruits you shall know dem." "Chilleren," he said, "what you done come here for? Yo' ole mammy wid de misery in yo' knees an' only a few mo' steps to toddle; yo' sinner man sittin' on de seats of do-nuffin'; yo' pearl young niggers songunnery in yo' views an' mighty stroblous in carryin' on 'em out, — what you done come here for?"

"We'se come to git religion," replied a voice from the benches.

"Praise de Lord!" replied the preacher, "praise de Lord if dat am so! Now, how yo' gwine to get it? What yo' reckon religion am, anyhow? Chill'en, jus yo' listen to me, an' I'll tell yo'. Dis yere am a fruit-growin' country; an' from de many 'lusions to vineyards an' fruit-trees, I reckon dat Jerusalem was a fruit-packin' town, pretty much d' same kine of a place as Oceola, an' in de country roun' dare was lots of orange plantations, jes' as yo' see 'em here. Leastways, de Marster he was always talkin' about de fruit business. And when he tried to 'splain what religion was, he tole 'em it was fruit-raisin'. Sez he, 'When I sets out a little seedlin', I don't

AT THE CAMP-MEETING.

'spect no fruit on it the fust year; but I nusses it up tree, five, sebben year, an' graffs it, an' buds it, and *den* ef it don't bear no fruit I cuts it down. It's nuffin' but a cucumber ob de groun'.' De Marster been more patient wid mose of yo' brederen an' sisteren dan dat.

How ole is yo', Libery Johnson? Is n't yo' more 'n sebben years ole? An' what kine of fruit yo' done b'ar fo' de Marster? Nuffin' but a crop of mons'ous wild grapes, wid yo' sky-larkin' about to balls, an' yo' begrudgefulness ob fine close, an' yo' triflin', simple carr'in's-on. 'Spec' de Marster sen' along Gabriel pretty soon wid a big axe to chop yo' down fo' fiahwood, — only yo' too green for dat, eben.

"Yo', Maum Phyllis, what fruit yo' been b'arin' fo' de Marster all dese years? What kine ob fruit is dem wrong tales yo' done tole 'bout your neighbors? An' yo' meanness, an' uncomfor'bleness to your fam'ly? I calls dat a crop ob de sourress kine ob persimmons, I does. What kine ob a face you reckon de Marster gwine to make when he tas'e 'em? But doan you cry an' lament yo' undone case, Maum Phyllis. Dar am hope fo' you. When de fross come, den de persimmons sweeten up; an' de fross ob ole age am a-grizzlin' yo' ha'r, an' de snow ob deff a-beatin' on de soundin'-post ob yo' head. See to it dat yo' persimmonses — I means your words an' yo' actions — is a sweet'nin' under dat fross fo' de Marster.

"Yo', Daddy Tucker, what fruit yo' done b'ar? Yo' is a church-member what pray mighty loud in de class-room fur de widder an' de orphanless, an' yo prays pretty much like dis, — 'O Lord, gibbin' doth not impoverish thee, neither doth withholdin' enrich thee; but gibbin' doth impoverish us, an' withholdin' doth enrich us; darfore yo' shell out, good Lord, an' hulp dis yere case.' What sorter fruit yo' t'ink yo' am? Yo', sah, am a water-million, mighty roun' an' promissin' to de eye, but so green an' hard at heart as not fitten to gib de pigs.

"Yo', Mrs. Aristotle Williams, yo' need n't shout 'Glory!' an' be so tickled at what I juss said. Yo' allus wants yo' name to head ebery perscription, whedder it am to fricassee de church or to raffle fo' a prize turkey. Yo' likes to come teeterin' up to de altar fibe times durin' meetin' wid yo' contribution, 'stead ob sendin' up a quarter by de Deacon oncet fo' all. Yo' so meally-moufed talkin' 'bout yo' sperit-ual 'speriences one would tink you jus' ready for to sprout yo' wings.

An' whar yo' done git dat money yo' make such a show ob gibbin' to de Lord? 'Spect dose pullets what Mister Brown loss might tell sumfin' 'bout it. Do yo' know what kine o' fruit yo' words an' actions is like? Yo' words is like a great ober-ripe pawpaws, soff as sqush; and yo' actions is like rotten bananers what makes one sick to counterplate.

"But, sisteren and brudderen, I see many a saint here who's borne fruit fo' de Lord ob a diff'ren' market-value from dat,— good, profitable trees in de nursery ob divine grace, what hab gone on quietly raisin' fruit all dese years. An' dat fruit it am canned an' preserbed an' pickled 'gainst dat great day. 'Pears like I has a sight into de store-room ob hebben, an' I sees de shelbs jus' a-groanin' wid tumblers ob guava jelly, an' jars ob brandied peaches, an' preserbed figs, an' marmalade just candied wid de sugar ob righteousness and lub, an' growin' sweeter an' sweeter wid de ages. De good book says, ' By dere fruit you shall know dem.' An' I 'pears to see de labels on dose jars : ' Sister Milly's Strawberry Jam,' — dat was de good deed she done all unbeknownst to any one; ' Brudder Pete's preserbed ginger,' — and nobody but de Lord an' Pete know wid what self-sacrifice dat ginger-root was done made fit for de Marster's table.

"Brudderen an' sisteren, let us all go home to our fruit-raisin', an' may we all be preserbed at last! Dat's what de good book say, — '.De Lord *preserbe* you;' but, sinnah, you'se got to tote up some sort ob fruit dat's worf preserbin'. De conflagration will now join in singin'—

'What kine ob slippers do de angels wear
As dey walks about on de upper air?'"

Cleopatra had been choking with suppressed merriment; but as they walked back to the hotel Madeleine said: " I don't see how you can laugh. There is real truth in it, after all. It is only a homely amplification of the Master's thought. I 'm afraid, Cleo, that all the fruit I have ever borne would make an infinitesimally small pot of jam."

"WRIGGLING OUT FROM UNDER A MASS OF TREE ROOTS."

"Why, Madeleine," said Cleopatra, "you are shivering! And how cold your hands are!"

"Oh, no," replied the young girl; "I am burning up. Just place your hand on my forehead."

"She is feverish," said Cleopatra. "Dr. Pettyman, do you think she is going to be sick?"

The Doctor felt her pulse, and drew her shawl more closely about her. "She has a chill," he said. "The night air of this swampy district is really dangerous."

"I am glad mother did not come out," moaned Madeleine. "Oh, my head, my head!"

They hastened home. Quinine and other remedies were found; and the next morning, as Madeleine was decidedly better, it was determined to start on their return trip down the Ocklawaha.

The Doctor was assiduous in his attentions; but no opportunity was given him to continue the topic which he had broached as they came up the river. The glamour was gone; and the whole effect of the scenery was very different by garish daylight. Still, there was a wild beauty and strangeness about it which was very fascinating. What was before only a confused and shadowy mass now showed itself in all the detail of luxuriant tropical foliage. "The Critter," who stood in the bow of the boat, kept a good look-out for alligators; and the Doctor handed Madeleine his revolver, that she might be ready for a shot when "The Critter" gave the signal. At length the sharp eyes of the old hunter descried one wriggling out from under a mass of tree roots, and Madeleine and Cleopatra both "shot at it" at the same time. Cleopatra was the more successful; for while Madeleine's bullets plashed harmlessly into the water, Cleopatra's shot with her detective camera gave her a good photograph of the great saurian. (See the frontispiece.)

Later in the afternoon Madeleine went down to the lower deck with Uncle Jonah to see "The Critter's" collection of baby alligators.

The conversation immediately turned to Yulee Ponce. "She's a likely girl," said "The Critter," "and plucky as she is likely. When the 'Yellow Jack' raged in St. Augustine, and every one was pulling up stakes and clearing the country, her mother and she stayed by. Mrs. Ponce, she was one of the best nusses we had. She was sent for far and near; and she was at it day and night till, just as the fever seemed to be leaving the town, down she come herself; and then the old man took it. He's part Injun, an' that accounts for his bein' so queer and quiet like, — lazy, some folks call him; but see him in the woods an' you would n't think him lazy. But he's sorter used to giving up, an' he giv' right up when the fever struck him. Yulee, she nussed her mother and father through it, and she wa'n't but a little slip of a gal then, only ten year old. Well, sir, if you'll believe me, she never took it; and her mother got well, though she had it the wuss kind, — all the bad symptoms, except the vomito and the 'mieux de mort.' Yaller? I see her one day — I did their markettin' for 'em — an' she was as yaller as a pumpkin. There's a sailor sick now in St. Augustine with something like yellow fever. He come from Demarara in that very schooner that we went to Anastasia Island in. They're trying to keep it hushed up for fear there'll be a panic. The man boarded with some folks that lived in a house that belongs to Mr. Tait. When he was taken sick they just up and scooted, — just cleared for the North, leavin' the poor feller alone in the house. Mr. Tait, he heard of it, and he drove right over to Mrs. Ponce's and got her to move in and nuss him. She's there now, I reckon. I see Ponce 'fore I come away. He said the man had the jarndice; but you can't fool me. If they called it yellow fever, there'd be the biggest scatterment from the hotels ever you see."

Madeleine was interested. "Is yellow fever contagious?" she asked.

"Well, some say 't is, and some ag'in say 't is n't. I've know it to be taken by men who went on board ships to clean 'em out. Clothes

FLYING SQUIRRELS.

give it sometimes; and sometimes nusses can take care of the wuss cases and never catch it. It's cur'us, it is."

Madeleine went to her state-room, and opening her toilet-case took out the fine soft sponge which she had obtained on the schooner. She had already used it in bathing, having first washed it until not a particle of the musty odor which had at first clung to it could be perceived; but now she dropped both the sponge and the bathing-case from her state-room window with an expression of horror. Then she sat down, and holding her head in her hands tried hard to think.

She had been exposed to yellow fever; of this she was certain. Could it be that her shivering fits were the premonitory symptoms of this dread disease? She did not care greatly for herself; but the rest, and above all her mother, must be shielded. Her thoughts would not come readily, and her head ached as though a heavy weight were pressing it down. Some plan must be resolved upon at once, and yet she could not think.

Cleopatra was calling her, and confused and dismayed she went on deck. The others pointed out the flying squirrels which were leaping from limb to limb among the trees on the shore. There seemed to be a colony of them emigrating from one locality to another.

"Will you shoot at them?" asked the Doctor.

"No, indeed," Madeleine replied. "The pretty little creatures have as much right to their lives as I have to mine. My heart reproaches me for even firing at that old alligator. He must lead such a pleasurable, cool, oozy existence in this shady aquarium!"

Her hands were burning, and it seemed to her at the moment that the alligator's haunt must be the most enviable place in the world. She took a book and seated herself on the little after-deck, where no wandering wind could blow from her toward any one of the party. Here she insured solitude for a time by pretending to read, while she vainly tried to puzzle out a course of action.

As they neared Palatka, the Doctor, who had discovered her retreat, came to her, and began to touch once more upon the subject to which he had alluded on their voyage up the river. Madeleine only vaguely comprehended what he was saying.

"You do not answer me," he said at last. "Surely such a question deserves a reply."

"I beg your pardon," she said, with a start. "But what were you saying?"

The Doctor bit his lip and colored. "I said that I would give my life for you, and asked you to allow me to pledge my utmost devotion to your service."

THE JUSTICE OF THE PEACE.

It was out at last, and the Doctor could not have proposed in a better time. Even the romance of the theatrical surroundings of the night voyage were as nothing to her present great need.

She looked at him with dry, glittering eyes. "You say you would risk your life for me?"

He thought her manner tragic, but responded effusively, "Certainly, with the utmost pleasure."

"I may test your offer," she replied. "Wait; I will give you my answer by and by."

A benevolent-appearing individual with elephantine ears now approached them, and remarked: "I live here at Palatka. I'm a justice of the peace, and would be glad to be of any service to you during your stay."

Madeleine looked at him uncomprehendingly, and walked away. The Doctor replied: "We are not meditating any offence against the public peace."

The man's smile rippled all over his features. "Oh no, sir; I should say not, sir. I have watched you with a fatherly interest, so to speak, during the entire voyage. I hope you'll excuse the remark, sir. I only mention it because there's another justice at Palatka, and he charges fifty cents more for marrying a couple than I do."

At another time the Doctor would have taken offence; but he saw that the man did not mean to be insulting, and he was very happy, — for he had told her, and she had not rejected him.

The confusion of arrival at Palatka now broke up all conversation. Madeleine, with her mortal secret locked behind her usual calmness, walked rapidly somewhat in advance of the rest to the hotel. They had planned to spend the night here; but at the office a telegram was handed to Mrs. Morse. "Your father has sprained his ankle," she said to Madeleine. "He wants me to come home directly."

A sudden light swept across the girl's face. "Of course you must go, and at once! Poor papa, how he needs you!"

"But I can't go yet," said Uncle Jonah. "I promised Mr. Tait to take a little trip with him to look at land before we went North."

"And I must see Yulee Ponce again, and help her for a week or two to fit her for Vassar," said Madeleine; "but that will not hinder Aunt Pen and mother and Cleopatra going right on to-night to Jacksonville, and taking the train for the North to-morrow. Uncle Jonah and I can follow you soon."

Aunt Pen, who was tired of sweet-potato pie and longed for her customary six desserts, was very willing to return to the North. Captain Saunters had disappointed her, and she considered him unworthy the privations she had endured in his behalf.

Cleopatra looked at Madeleine with a pained wonder. "I would rather stay with you," she said; "and I think you are downright unkind to post me off in this way."

"Yes," urged Mrs. Morse, "Pen and I will make our way very nicely, and I think it would be better for your friend to stay with you."

While the others were at dinner Madeleine took Cleopatra out upon the piazza. "Cleo," she said, "I wish you would trust me for once. I want you to go with Mamma; I cannot tell you the reason, but our friendship ought to stand as much as that."

Cleo wound an arm around the resisting girl. "Something is the matter with you, Madeleine; you don't act like yourself. I believe you need me, and I am going to stay."

Madeleine twisted herself out of her friend's embrace. "You *must* go, Cleo," she whispered; "it may be death for you to remain. Look at my face and hands!"

"Oh, that's it!" Cleopatra replied coolly, evidently much relieved. "You are sick; then of course you want me. I have been watching that viperous little Doctor, and I thought he had something to do with your lunacy. Yulee and I will take care of you, and we will have you well in no time."

"But don't you see? can't you understand? It is yellow fever, Cleo, and you have no right to endanger yourself. Don't breathe a syllable of this to mother, but get her away to-night. I will go to Yulee. Her mother is a trained nurse; they will take me in, and I shall be well cared for."

Cleopatra looked very serious, but she did not falter. "I don't believe it's any such thing. You are a little bilious, that's all; but if it were small-pox I'd stay by you just the same. Now, don't make any fuss about it, or I'll betray the entire scheme."

The Doctor approached, with Aunt Pen's orders to bring the young ladies to supper. "Will you kindly escort mother and Aunt Pen to Jacksonville," asked Madeleine, "and see them started for the North? We will spend the night here, and go on with Uncle Jonah to-morrow to St. Augustine."

"Where I trust I may have the privilege of seeing you," said the Doctor.

In the hurry of Mrs. Morse's leave-taking Madeleine's appearance was not commented upon until just as her mother parted from her she said, " Do be careful of yourself, dear child, and don't study too hard ; you are looking very badly."

Madeleine murmured that it was only a headache ; and Cleopatra cried assuringly, as the boat left the dock, that she would take good care of Madeleine and give her " loads of quinine."

CHAPTER IX.

IN THE FURNACE.

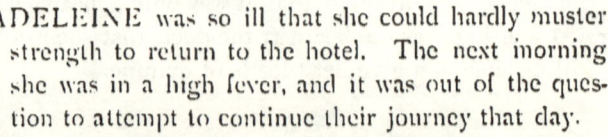ADELEINE was so ill that she could hardly muster strength to return to the hotel. The next morning she was in a high fever, and it was out of the question to attempt to continue their journey that day.

Uncle Jonah was not greatly alarmed. "You've got a touch of the ague," he said; and he administered a large dose of quinine, foretelling that she would be better on the morrow.

And Uncle Jonah was right. The fever was evidently of a remittent type; and the next day, though quite weak, Madeleine was able to go on to St. Augustine.

Madeleine held up bravely before Uncle Jonah, who bade her good-by in Yulee's little shop, as he intended to leave town early the next morning on his Indian River expedition. The good man had no idea how very ill his niece was; but he shook her kindly by the hand, and told her to be careful of herself. Madeleine smiled feebly, but did not return her uncle's kiss; and when he had crossed the street to his hotel she turned to Yulee with a piteous expression, and tried to speak, but found it impossible. Overtaxed nature asserted itself, and she sank fainting into Yulee's arms.

The two girls carried her into Yulee's room, and laid her upon the little bed. "It is but just to you," said Cleopatra, "for me to tell you that she probably has the yellow fever. It is very possible that you would rather we should be isolated in some other house. Money is of no consequence at such a time as this, but there are some things which even money cannot buy."

Yulee stopped her. "You say right, money is of no consequence. I take her not for ze money, but for love. I know all; see have write me, — I have justly receive the letter. I will nurse her so careful. You need not to cry; see sall not die."

"But your shop — who will take care of it?"

"Ze shop can be close; or if you will, if you would like to be near, you can mind ze shop. You know you cannot stay wiz your friend. I have had ze fever. I have no danger; but you —"

"I cannot leave her," Cleopatra replied hurriedly. "I have been already exposed; it does not matter."

"You do not understand ze danger; it is not ze contagion of seeing one time or two time in ze day, it is to stand alway over ze sick person. You may come to her sometimes, but you can help much more to do ze outside errand, — to go for ze doctor, ze medeseen, ze necessaires. If you could now go for my muzzer it would help much more as to stand here."

"I will go," Cleopatra replied obediently.

The two girls seemed to have exchanged natures. Cleopatra wilful, commanding, was suddenly docile and meek; and little Yulee Ponce, the wistful, timid girl, assumed the generalship of the situation by the divine right of knowing just the thing which should be done, combined with the will and power to do it.

Cleopatra hurried through the darkening streets to the little house where Mrs. Ponce was nursing the sick sailor.

She heard Cleopatra's startling news with a calmness which the girl mistook for stolidity. "Tell her," she said, "zat my man is besser. I fine some uzzer to nurse him; I come home to-morrow."

Cleopatra next went for a physician. The one whom Yulee had

recommended was out; and leaving a note for him, she hurriedly ordered ice and made a few other purchases, returning home so weary that she could scarcely stand.

Yulee heard her report with interest. "And now you must take some repose to yourself," she said. "Look! see does sleep. I will sit wiz her zee night; see does not require you."

Cleopatra looked at Madeleine. She was indeed asleep, though from time to time she tossed and moaned uneasily. She opened her eyes as her friend kissed her. "Cleo," she said, "if I should die, tell Captain Saunters — " Then the lids fell, and the rest ended in an inarticulate murmur.

"What shall I tell him, dear?" Cleopatra asked; but Yulee placed her finger on her lip.

"Hush!" she said; "see sleep, see must not be disturb; it is ze only hope." Then with a strong, steady hand she led the unwilling girl from the room.

"I will lie down on the lounge here," Cleopatra consented, "and you must call me if you need me."

She thought she would close her eyes for only a few moments, but it was broad daylight before the wearied girl awoke. There was an appetizing odor of coffee, and Mrs. Ponce looked in to say, "Ze breakfass, he is ready."

It was Madeleine's bad day, and the fever was now at its height. She was delirious, and talked wildly and incoherently, now of their trip up the Ocklawaha, now of the camp-meeting and the negro minister's sermon, and again of their plans for Yulee's education; and here she seemed most sane. "I wrote him," she said, "that I did not want his help for Yulee, I would do it all myself; and now if I am going to die, I can't. 'Fruit fo' de Marster, — what fruit yo done bore fo' de Marster?' Apples of Sodom, fair to look upon, but ashes to the taste, — only ashes! Ice, ice! please give me more ice! See the alligators! what a nice, cool, lovely time they are having in the shady water! Oh, Patrick, please tell Captain Saunters! You will, won't you, Cleo dear?"

And again Cleopatra asked, her heart wrung with anguish, "What shall I say to him, Madeleine darling?" But Madeleine could not tell.

The doctor had not come, and Cleopatra went out in search of him. He was at home now; but when he understood the nature of the disease, he refused to take charge of the case. Disappointed and troubled, she turned from the door. To whom could she apply?

Just then a carriage passed her, turned, and drove to meet her. It was Dr. Pettyman, looking in the large barouche, as she afterward remarked, like a very small kernel rattling about in a very large nutshell. He alighted briskly, and said that he had but just arrived in St. Augustine, having seen Mrs. Morse and her sister well started for the North. "And now," he remarked effusively, "what can I do for the regal Cleopatra and the charming Miss Madeleine? I am entirely at your service; name but your orders, and I fly to execute them."

Cleopatra looked at the smirking little man; she was very averse to applying to him, and yet he was a physician and their need was great. "Dr. Pettyman," she said, "we are in great trouble; Madeleine is very ill."

Instantly the shrewd little man comprehended that here was another opportunity. "Step right into the carriage," he said, "and take me to her. I am only too thankful to be of the slightest aid."

Relieved and grateful, Cleopatra, as they rode, told him the entire story; and as she did so the expression of the Doctor's countenance changed. "Yellow fever!" he gasped; "that puts a very different face on the matter. You ought to have a specialist, some one who has had experience in the disease;" and he named a noted physician.

"He is not in St. Augustine."

"Then Dr. ———."

"He has refused to take the case."

"Dr. —— refused! Then it must be a malignant case;" and he inquired minutely into the symptoms. The carriage stood before the door, and Cleopatra sprang out; but the Doctor hesitated. "I have an important engagement," he stammered.

"Surely nothing more important than this! Dr. Pettyman, you are not going to desert us!"

'Desert you? Oh no, but I think I had better drive around to the hotel for my medicine case. I will be back soon;" and without entering the house Dr. Pettyman was gone.

Madeleine was, if possible, worse; her cries for water were piteous. Mrs. Ponce fed her with chopped ice patiently. Yulee had lain down for a little rest. There seemed to be nothing to do until the Doctor came; and Cleopatra went into the shop, and patiently showed feather and palm work to the tourists who happened in, and sold sea-beans and pressed algæ in a dazed way, often making wrong change. People wondered who that refined-looking shop-girl was, who was so very stupid in her arithmetic. No one came in whom she knew, excepting the little darky with flowers, which she purchased and carried in to Madeleine.

The sick girl opened her eyes languidly. "Did you tell him?" she asked.

"Tell who? tell what?" Cleopatra urged; but the question only set her into wilder delirium. And still the Doctor did not come. A little past noon a messenger brought Cleopatra a note.

DEAR MISS ATCHISON,— I am telegraphed for; important business calls me suddenly to the North. I am sorry not to be able to remain and devote myself to Miss Morse. I trust she will endure this severe ordeal. Her remarkable constitution is on her side.

With deepest regret, hastily yours, J. PETTYMAN.

A smile of fine scorn curled Cleopatra's lip. The Doctor had proved himself a broken reed. She did not believe in the telegram; it was only a ruse. He was a coward, and had basely deserted them.

Meantime they must have medical advice. Mrs. Ponce asked her when she thought the Doctor would come, and she could hear Madeleine moaning. "Oh! what shall I do?" she cried impotently; "perhaps I had better telegraph for her mother, after all. It is just possible that her Uncle Jonah is still at the hotel. I will go and see."

But Uncle Jonah had left a few hours previous. Despairing, almost desperate, Cleopatra walked down the street. To whom could she apply? Oh for some old friend in whom she could trust!

CATHEDRAL AT ST. AUGUSTINE.

Suddenly the words of a hymn passed through her mind, —

"Human hearts and looks deceive me;
Thou art not, like them, untrue."

The doors of the old Spanish Cathedral, built so long ago, stood always open for prayer. She entered and knelt before the white shrine of Our Lady, and prayed earnestly for help. The silver lamp swung censer-like overhead; the coolness and quiet of the place refreshed her, and she came out determined to apply to every physician in the place, full of faith now that some one would be sent to help them.

Suddenly she was startled by an exclamation from some one in a dark doorway, and turning saw Captain Saunters. He stepped forward eagerly, with such a look of delight that Cleopatra had not the heart to rebuff him. "You don't look much like an angel," she said, "but perhaps the Lord has sent you all the same. Can you tell me of some physician with conscience enough not to refuse a dangerous case?"

The young man's face blanched. "Is Miss Madeleine sick?"

"Yes; yellow fever. You look frightened; every one is. I don't ask you to come near us, only to direct me to some doctor."

"But I shall come near you, and I am not afraid except for her. Where are you stopping?"

"At Yulee's."

"I will be there in fifteen minutes with our surgeon; he has had experience in the very worst epidemics."

"TURNING, SHE SAW CAPTAIN SAUNTERS."

And the Captain was as good as his word. In seventeen minutes he strode through the curiosity shop with the surgeon, — a sphinx in spectacles, which took all expression from his eyes, and gave you the feeling that he wore them to mask his opinions.

Who admitted him or how it happened, Cleopatra did not know; but Captain Saunters stood beside the bed, while the Doctor made his diagnosis.

Madeleine recognized him, and asked, "Cleo told you?"

"Yes," said the Doctor; and aside to the Captain, "Say yes; keep her mind easy."

"It is all right," the Captain replied cheerily, though his voice trembled. She put out her thin yellow hand, and he took it reverently.

"Now go away," said the surgeon; "you bother me."

He went into the shop, where Cleopatra was showing dried grasses to a customer. When the lady had gone he asked, "What was it she wanted you to tell me?"

"I do not know," Cleopatra replied, with tears in her eyes; "perhaps we can find out to-morrow."

The Captain came and went, bringing comforts. Cleopatra found him a great help. He did not again attempt to penetrate farther than the little shop, but she knew it was from delicacy and not from cowardice. It was strange that what had incensed her so much no longer troubled her. She did think of it, but with that divine forgiveness which gentle women exercise so inconsistently, now condoning the worst faults and at other times visiting the merest peccadillo with merciless severity. Having determined to pardon the Captain, she did so thoroughly. Her instinct

"A SPHINX IN SPECTACLES."

told her that he was to be trusted; and so, though her judgment condemned him, woman-like she allowed her instinct to lead her in spite of her judgment, and in so doing did not err. Her self-reliance too, or rather her reliance on God, returned. He had not left them friendless; and she made her change with exactitude, and attended to the little business with cheerfulness and despatch. as though she had been brought up in it. At night Madeleine's temperature was lower, and she rested more comfortably. The next day it intermitted, as usual; and the surgeon asked more questions, and studied the case more carefully, fixing his astute, impenetrable gaze now on his patient and now on Cleopatra. Madeleine was too weak to talk much, and she did not refer to the topic which troubled her in her delirious moments. She looked up once as Cleopatra bent over her, and asked, "Have you written my mother? Does she know?"

"No," replied Cleopatra; "and I shall not do so unless you are worse."

A smile of infinite content came into Madeleine's face. "Mother must not be troubled," she said.

Cleopatra told the Doctor the sick girl's earnest desire that her mother should not be alarmed. "I am afraid, sir," she said, "that I may be doing wrong in yielding to her wishes. If her life is in danger her mother ought to be sent for. Tell me, please, if you think she should be informed."

"You need not telegraph at present," the Doctor replied; "I think we are going to pull her through."

This was encouraging so far as it went; but the next day Madeleine was worse, — as it seemed to Cleopatra, very much worse. Her delirious talk was all of the Heavenly City and of friends who had passed away. She sang feebly snatches of the weird songs which they had heard at the camp-meeting.

> "My sister's gone to Heaven,
> And I want to go too,
> For to try on the long white robes,
> Chilleren!
> For to try on the long white robes."

And again,

> "Oh! what kind of slippers does de angels wear,
> As dey walks about on de upper air?"

She was not quite sane on her well day, when there was no fever, and talked strangely of an angel or to one, — Cleopatra could not make out exactly which. Several days passed by in this way, Cleopatra suffering the keenest anxiety. She wrote to Mrs. Morse that Madeleine was not well; but the good lady had no suspicion of the furnace through which the girls were passing.

CHAPTER X.

CROSSING THE BRIDGE.

ADELEINE was in a strange mental condition. It seemed to her that she had suffered as much as she could endure, and she prayed eagerly for release. Death or life, no matter which, — only take away this intolerable pain, this thirst unquenchable, with the noise of rushing waters forever in her ears. Suddenly something seemed to snap in her brain, and there was a great calm.

> "The sickness, the nausea,
> The pitiless pain,
> Had ceased with the fever
> That maddened her brain,
> With the fever called 'Living,'
> That burned in her brain."

How glad, how thankful, she was that it was all over! Not for worlds would she lie down upon that bed again and renew the struggle! Her life had been short indeed, but joyous and void of any trouble; she had escaped the evil days of later years. "Whom the gods love, die young," she said; and she thought herself very fortunate. It seemed to her that though she had died, her spirit still flitted about under the gray coquina arches of the old Spanish house. She was not shod with the angelic slippers, and could not climb the

"A TALL ANGEL STOOD BENEATH IT."

starry stair. Her feet were heavy, and when she strove to lift them, dragged upon the stone-flagging. Why was it, she wondered, that she could not go? She wandered in spirit out through the cool, shady corridors into the glowing garden. The sunshine fell hot upon the dried-up fountain over which scarlet cacti were clambering. There was a palm at the lower end of the garden, and she drifted toward it, and strove to break off a branch; but a tall angel stood beneath it, who lifted his hand in warning.

"First earn your palm," he said. "Where are the fruits which your life has borne?"

"How could I bear fruit?" she replied. "I have died too young. What opportunity have I had?"

"What opportunity?" repeated the angel; and he pointed to Yulee, who sat braiding palm-strands.

"She is weeping," said Madeleine; "she at least is sorry that I have gone."

"Her tears are not those of grateful remembrance," replied the angel. "She is weeping over disappointed hopes. You promised to help her to an education, did you not?"

"I should have made provision for her," Madeleine, or Madeleine's ghost, replied, "but I was cut down too suddenly."

"There was some one else who was willing to help you in your good work," continued the angel.

"I was angry with him," the poor ghost replied, "and wrote him that I did not need his help, — that I preferred to do it all myself."

"What right had you to refuse what was not to be your own, and to leave promises unfulfilled?"

"I had no right," Madeleine's ghost answered humbly; "let me go now and haunt him until he understands that he is to continue my work."

The angel shook his head in pity. "Poor child," he said, "how little you understand! He would not be conscious of your presence if you haunted him, as you call it, for years. Many spirits flit about the world, but the eyes of the living are holden, — they cannot see. Then, too, he could not do your work for you. He has his own duty to perform; opportunities are sometimes given us but once, and they are often given to but one person. It was yours while you lived to aid this young girl, and to influence others to aid her; now that you are dead, your aid and influence have alike ceased."

"There have been people," pleaded Madeleine, "whose influence lived after them. I am sure that he remembers me, and would gladly do something in my memory. Let me try at least."

The angel sorrowfully bowed his head; and Madeleine floated out of the garden down King Street, which was bordered with live-oak and hung with Spanish moss. No one noticed her as she passed; and she hastened on to the sea-wall, where she had loved to walk. There were the quay and the pretty club-house. There were the yachts, their white wings folded waiting for the approaching regatta.

Madeleine's spirit skimmed along the promenade till she found a lonely man sitting in an angle of the wall looking away to seaward. It was the Captain, and Madeleine knew by a strange spiritual intuition that he was thinking of her. "She will die," thought the Captain; and Madeleine's ghost heard the thought as distinctly as though it were a spoken word. "How lovely, how good, she was! how kind to every one, even to poor little Yulee Ponce!"

"No, no!" cried Madeleine, passionately. "I meant to be good, I meant to be kind, but I put it off. You wanted to help me; will you not take up the work where I left it?"

"I was not worthy to help her," thought the Captain, "but I shall be a better man for having known such a perfect being."

"Perfect!" wailed the ghost. "What kindly derision it is! But he says he will be a better man. I wonder what he *will* do for my sake; will he not think of helping Yulee?"

And Saunters, as though in answer to her question, thought on: "She was so cultured, so intellectual, such a contrast to Yulee, I wonder that I could ever have been charmed by that little ignoramus.

'And though she was not learned, — well,
I was not anxious she should grow so.
I trembled once beneath her spell,
Whose spelling was extremely so-so.'

But Madeleine has shown me what a woman ought to be. I shall never go near Yulee again. Let her develop into a coarse stupid woman like her mother; it is nothing to me."

Madeleine's ghost wailed and wrung her hands. This, then, was all that her memory and influence had done with the Captain. Up there in the North she knew that her mother would grieve sincerely. There was some money that was to have been her own; what would be done with it? She seemed to see her father and mother talking about it together. Her mother wore expensive crapes, and there was a look of deep sorrow on her father's face.

"I never want to touch a penny of Madeleine's money," he said; "it shall all be expended in a monument to her memory. What do you think she would have liked?"

"Madeleine had a very fastidious taste," Mrs. Morse remarked. "Here is a drawing which she made of Yulee Ponce holding a palm-branch; it only needs wings to make a lovely angel. Is it not a most artistic thing?"

"I will try to get one of our best sculptors to carve it. What do you say to St. Gaudens?" asked Mr. Morse.

Madeleine's ghost groaned.

"Madeleine was very fond of Vassar," suggested Mrs. Morse; "perhaps she would have liked something for the college."

"Mother, darling mother!" cried the ghost in joyful ecstasy; "you at last are going to guess just what I want."

"Very well," replied Mr. Morse, in a satisfied tone which implied that he hit upon exactly the right thing. "We will have it cut as a bas-relief, and placed as a memorial tablet somewhere about Vassar College."

The poor disappointed ghost heard no more; even those dearest and nearest could not imagine what she would have had done. As she drifted back toward the South it seemed to her that she saw Dr. Pettyman, and that he was reading the notice of her death in a paper. "Dead!" the Doctor thought, "how very fortunate! now she will never know that I refused to act as her physician." There was one friend left who she knew was true and who comprehended her aims. This was Cleopatra; but Cleo was poor and could do nothing for Yulee. The angel was right; the same opportunity was rarely given to but one person. Yulee had been her opportunity of fruit-bearing, and she had missed it.

The angel stood before her again, grave and questioning. "Does your aid and influence live after you?" he asked.

"Not as I would have them," she cried. "Oh, let me go back and finish the work which I meant to do!"

"That is a boon seldom granted," replied the angel.

But Madeleine struggled with the spirit, as Jacob wrestled with the mysterious stranger, until even he was moved by her strong pleading which was not for herself. "I am Israfil," he said, "sent to release you from the suffering which you were enduring. Are you willing to take it up once more,—to lie down and battle for your life with the fever?"

Madeleine's spirit shuddered, then replied calmly, "I am willing."

Then a sharp pain shot through her brain, and she was conscious that she was lying again on Yulee's bed, and that the strange surgeon with the spectacles was looking at her thoughtfully, and speaking in a low voice to Cleopatra.

"Yes; she has been and still is a very sick woman, but it is not yellow fever. It is never intermittent, and this, you see, is another of her good days. Weak as she is, she is not delirious. I see by the clear light in her eyes that she knows us, and I believe she is going to recover."

"Yes," replied Madeleine, gravely, "I am going to get well."

She closed her eyes, for she was very weary. Yulee lifted her in her arms, and gave her something nourishing to drink; and then she slept,—slept long and dreamlessly, all through that day and night on into the following day, which should have been that of the fever.

Toward evening she awoke much refreshed. The crisis was passed, and she was saved. This was what the surgeon said, and Madeleine repeated the word "saved." Yes, saved from her old, scornful, careless self. She had wakened from her delirium with all her better impulses strengthened, with a new view of the seriousness of life and an appreciation of its uncertainty, of the little time at the best given us for our work here and the importance of doing that work at once and thoroughly. Though sweetly serious, she was not saddened by her grave experience. The world looked far more beautiful to her than ever before. As she lay in the hammock under the cool arches of the corridor during her days of convalescence and looked out at the garden, a keen appreciation of its picturesqueness swept over her. "America is beautiful, after all," she said to Cleopatra. "I have never seen anything more lovely than this in Europe. I take back all the dreadful things which I said before we started on this journey. St. Augustine and that trip up the Ocklawaha have converted me."

FEEDING THE CHICKENS.

"But this garden and the southern Florida jungle are all tropical in character," Cleopatra objected. "Are you sure that what you admire in them is not their very foreign feeling, and not the distinctive American character?"

"No," replied Madeleine; "it is all beautiful. Could anything be more American than that Southern girl in her sun-bonnet in the next yard feeding her chickens, and yet she is just as picturesque to me as a European peasant, and her face is far more interesting. Even that shambling negro adds the element of the grotesque. I wonder that I never noticed it before. Is it possible that it is the new joy which I feel in being alive once more which tinges everything with loveliness?"

Madeleine always spoke as if she had really died, and had been restored to life. Now that it was all over, she wrote a long letter to her mother telling her the entire story, and explaining her wishes in regard to Yulee. Madeleine felt that her time now was not her own. Perhaps she had been sent back just to make plain about Yulee's education, and might have a relapse and be snatched away at any moment. At any rate, she determined to leave nothing undone which she might lament in case of such an event. "Do the most important duties first," was her motto ever after. Many crowded days were hers in after life, when she could not possibly accomplish all which it seemed to her desirable to be done; but on the morning of such a day she sent a quick, prayerful, discriminating glance forward to the end, and told herself which were the most important duties.

A SHAMBLING NEGRO.

"Cleo," she said one day, "I would like to speak with Captain Saunters. Has he never called?"

"Every day, dear, to inquire or leave something. I asked him yesterday if he did not wish to see you, and he said, 'Very much, but perhaps I ought to wait till she is better; she will let me know when I can come.' I think, Madeleine, that he fancies that his presence would not be agreeable to you."

A faint flush tinged Madeleine's cheek. "I have treated him very badly," she said; and when the Captain called that afternoon she repeated the words, adding, "I owe you an apology, Captain Saunters. I have been a scornful, hasty girl. Will you forgive me?"

"Say only that you forgive me," replied the young man, much touched. "I have felt that possibly you did not understand just the real state of the case, or you might not have been so hard upon me. Still it was bad enough, and I do not know that any explanation can make it seem better."

"I would like to hear the entire story from you, nevertheless," Madeleine replied. "I shall not retract my forgiveness, whatever it may be."

And Saunters told it simply and truthfully, without sparing himself. Cleopatra's eyes grew large and indignant, for she too was listening. "Do you mean to say that this occurred only between yourself and Dr. Pettyman, and that there were no other witnesses?"

"We were quite alone."

"And the Doctor led me to believe that it was at the Club House, before a room full of amused witnesses, of whom he was one. Did you say that he challenged you to the bet?"

"He certainly was the first to suggest it; and though I thoughtlessly accepted the challenge at first, I immediately retired from it."

"In the same interview?"

"Almost in the same breath."

"Then," said Madeleine, "I do not see that in any true sense you really could be said to have made it."

"I thank you for that decision," replied the Captain, a great wave of pleasure sweeping over his features; "and now I can bear to tell you that I am ordered West. I leave next week, and could not have done so happily, without the knowledge that you were recovering, and that you had come once more to regard me as an honorable man."

They had one more interview, when their talk was principally of Yulee. Captain Saunters's gift toward her education was formally accepted by Madeleine. They spoke little of their own futures. His own was very uncertain. And though he knew now that he loved Madeleine devotedly, with this love there was mingled a great reverence; it was happiness enough to think that he stood before her acquitted, and further than this he did not dare to venture.

Madeleine wondered whether her dream of him were true, but after his generous gift to her in behalf of Yulee came to think that it was only a dream, and that he was still interested in the young Minorcan. "I will do all I can," she promised herself, "to make her a fit companion for him."

The evening ended delightfully under the arches. Cleopatra strummed gayly upon her guitar, and Yulee sang a little Spanish song,—

> "Si el amor del estudiante
> Fuera cosa permanente,
> No hubiera nada en el mundo
> Que fuera tan excelente."

"What does it mean?" Madeleine asked; and Yulee translated,—

"If see lofe of ze student man were something of permanency, zen nossing in ze world would be more besser."

"Ah!" exclaimed the Captain, "that is where the student man differs from the soldier man. I wonder how it is with the student girl?"

"He means Yulee, of course," thought Madeleine; "he must regard her already as a Vassar student."

And so the evening grew to night, and good-byes were said quite cheerfully, and without any sentimentality, but with a deep, true sentiment on the Captain's part, which was destined to be long unexpressed and misunderstood.

"Cleo," exclaimed Madeleine the next day, "how forgetful I am! I have not asked for Dr. Pettyman since I have been ill."

"Well, I wouldn't ask for him," Cleopatra replied snappishly.

"You never liked him, Cleo; still, as he is a physician, I wonder you did not call him in to treat me."

"It is one thing to call, and another to answer."

"And Dr. Pettyman—"

"Doesn't answer," replied Cleopatra, with a laugh. "I told him what we thought was the matter, and he found urgent business elsewhere. Captain Saunters was our only friend in need— Oh, yes" (thinking of her experience in the cathedral), "and the best Friend of All."

"You mean Yulee; I do not forget how much I owe her and her mother; but, Cleo, what puzzles me is this. I cannot understand how Dr. Pettyman, who has proved himself so untrustworthy, could have written such a book as 'Sir Galahad.'"

"He never wrote it," Cleopatra replied impulsively, looking up from the book which she happened to hold in her hand.

IN THE HAMMOCK.

"He said he did, Cleo; and because he has not told the truth in one instance, we cannot take it for granted that he is a literary forger."

"I do not know whether it is any baser to pretend to the writing of an insignificant little book like that than to desert you as he did. I only know that he did not write that book."

"It is not an insignificant little book, as you must admit, though that has nothing to do with the crime of wearing another's laurel; and you cannot know that he did not write it, Cleo, unless you also know who did."

"Very well, then, I do know, — *I* wrote it."

"Cleopatra Atchison!"

"Yes, dear, and it *is* insignificant. Its only merit is that it reproduces your thoughts, — ideas which I have heard you express from time to time, — and it is not complimentary to either of us to suggest it, but I fancy that is the reason you have cared for the book."

"No, indeed, I never had any ideas that were half so good. On the contrary, it has been an inspiration and a help to me. Do you know, Cleo, that you are a genius?"

"No, Madeleine, I shall never be an author. I wrote all I had to say in that one book, and cannot conceive of the possibility of ever writing another. I shall simply try to live up to my ideals now, instead of creating new ones."

Uncle Jonah came back from his trip, and was shocked to hear how ill his niece had been. "And to think you let me go away, when you supposed all the time that you had the yellow fever."

"But it was not the yellow fever, dear uncle; so you were spared a needless fright. It was a great joke on us all, was it not?"

"I don't know about that, — I don't know about that," he said, taking her thin hand in his. " I guess it was about as bad as it could be, Madeleine, without — " And here the old man's voice broke, for he loved his niece dearly. "I'll stay around here until you are ready to travel. There's going to be a regatta that I want to see. What do you say to yachting it back to New York? Oh! I forgot it was the cruise in the schooner that gave you the fever. Well, I'll charter a parlor-car, and will take you home the easiest way possible, as soon as the weather is too warm for you to stay longer."

"The surgeon does not think that I contracted my fever in the schooner or from the sponge which I carried away from it. He says that would have been the way to take yellow fever; but the sailor, the only one sick on board who was supposed to have brought it to St. Augustine, had something quite different, and it has turned out that there were no cases of yellow fever either here or in any of the ports from which the schooner had sailed, and my fever came from exposure to night air in malarial districts. So, dear uncle, if it is possible to return by sea, I think Patrick and I would like that way very much."

Very opportunely a friend was discovered on the point of returning to New York in a large yacht, with ample accommodations for Uncle Jonah and the three girls,—for it was decided that Yulee was to go with them. Her education had been so irregular that it was judged best to give her a preparatory course in a private school in New York before entering her for her special scientific one at Vassar.

Mrs. Ponce did not hesitate at the parting. She recognized the opportunity which was opening before her daughter, and she accompanied her to the steamer-landing proudly arrayed in her best, with a black silk shawl thrown mantilla-like over her head and shoulders, and giving her, as Cleopatra remarked, a decided likeness to Queen Isabella of Spain.

Raphael Ponce was there, too, shy and silent, with great tears rolling down his cheeks, for he felt by some dumb intuition that their parting was a final one. As he parted from his daughter he said simply, "Yulee go over bridge."

Madeleine remembered that "The Critter" had told her that he was part Indian; and one day, as they sat beneath the awning in the stern watching the long wake left by the boat on the smooth water, she asked Yulee if this were true.

"Fazzer all Indian," Yulee replied. "He Seminole; live when he little boy by Lake Flirt, away beyond ze Caloosahatchie River. His fazzer hunter and guide for gentlemans who travel. His muzzer when she little girl been take by Catholic priest to a school, learn speak Inglees, learn read. But see homesick, and see run away; journey long, long ways on foots and go home. Zen when see grow bigger, see marry my granfazzer; he talk Inglees too. By-and-by my fazzer be born. When he little boy his muzzer tell him about white peoples; he all time ask her to tell about zem. He hear his fazzer and muzzer talk Inglees, he crazy to learn it too. His fazzer take him with him in canoe down to ze settlements; he fery curious to stay zere. He not like uzzer Indian boy, he make his muzzer teach him read. Zen by-and-by he say, 'I go learn more white man's road. I not live in swamp like snake; I live in house.' Zen his muzzer, see make little bundle his clothes, bring him one day clear to settlement, ofer hill just where little bridge lead road to town. Zen see say, 'Zis side bridge Indian; uzzer side white peoples.' He pull her hand and say, 'Come wiz me;" but see say, 'Me no like zat side bridge,' and see kiss him and cry, and he come ofer. He come St. Augustine, and work earn his lifing. Sometimes he go back see his fazzer and muzzer. He like much once each year make camp in woods, but he have seen my muzzer when he first come to St. Augustine; zat keep him from be homesick for Indian life, and by-and-by my muzzer see marry him, and zey fery happy. But he get restless, — go off wander in wood. See much scare, for people tell her some time he go off so never come back no more. So next time he go in wood see go too. So we go efery year."

"This is all very interesting," said Madeleine. "Will you tell me what your father meant when he referred to the bridge as he bade you farewell? Was it the little bridge which you tell me he crossed when he determined to leave the old wild life?"

Yulee bowed her head. "When you come see me, be my friend, teach me, fazzer, he say, 'Yes, yes, all same you tired home life, want know more. Well, I no hinder.' I say, 'No, fazzer, I not tired, I not go way.' He say, 'Zat all right, by-and-by come bridge; you go over, I stay uzzer side.' He say, 'Zat all same right, only you must not forget poor old fazzer and muzzer.' So when I go away in boat he say, 'Now we come to ze bridge.'"

This then was the man whom Madeleine had thought stolid and unfeeling. He had shown himself appreciative of the opportunity offered his daughter, and although keenly sensitive, capable of sublime self-sacrifice; and he was an Indian. More than this, Yulee, to whom under God she owed her life, was of Indian blood. Surely there was something in the race capable of improvement. No one need tell her after this that it was useless to offer the Indian civilization; and while she determined to discharge as far as possible the debt which she owed Yulee personally, there came over her mind a dawning consciousness of the debt which we as a nation owe her people. She thought of her mother's active interest in foreign missions, while she had never heard her, or any of the philanthropic people whom she knew, speak of doing anything for these heathen at home, whom

PIER OF BROOKLYN BRIDGE.

we have driven farther and farther to the west, perfectly willing that they should live and die in barbarity so long as we possess their lands.

Dreaming thus, she was startled from her reverie by the exclamation of Cleopatra, "Is it not the noblest bridge in the world?" They were in New York harbor, and Cleopatra did not refer to the gangway held out by education to ignorance, but to the grand piers of the Brooklyn Bridge, which now loomed up before them.

CHAPTER XI.

WILD COLORADO.

AFTER her arrival in New York, Cleopatra returned to Vassar for the remainder of the school year, but found it impossible to graduate the following June. Perhaps she did not try very desperately, for she wished to remain in the same class with her friend.

When summer came her father wrote that he had obtained leave of absence from his New Mexican post for two months, and would meet her in Denver and take her on a grand Western tour; and he sincerely hoped that she would be able to induce Mrs. and Miss Morse to accompany her.

Madeleine's parents had been discussing plans for the summer. Mrs. Morse had been strongly in favor of Switzerland, for the family physician advised mountain air, as Madeleine had not entirely regained her strength; but her father disliked to have the ocean between them, and Madeleine herself did not care to go abroad. This invitation was accordingly greeted with enthusiasm. Mrs. Morse had become deeply attached to Yulee, and declared that she could not think of making this tour without her. Madeleine might be taken ill again, and no other nurse would possibly do. Yulee consented to accompany them in the capacity of maid; but this was only agreed to in order to make her mind easy on the score of expense, and she was treated in every way during the trip as an equal and a friend.

WILD COLORADO. 149

Early in July the four ladies set out by the Atchison, Topeka, and Santa Fé Railroad one of the pleasantest of western routes, and stopping only at St. Louis they found themselves in Colorado a little in advance of Major Atchison. It was therefore decided to wait for him

GATEWAY TO THE GARDEN OF THE GODS.

at Manitou — a delightful mountain-resort not far from Denver, and nestled just at the foot of Pike's Peak.

All the last day of their journey, as they rode westward, they strained their eyes for a glimpse of the Rockies. A bank of cloud lay provokingly low on the western horizon, piling up its cumulus masses in semblance of peaks. They knew that the mountains must be there, and again and again fancied that they saw them. Gradually the white changed to blue; and little by little the ranges outlined themselves, the summits alone still wrapped in mystery.

One bold mountain stood out in advance of the others so grandly and majestically that with one accord they all exclaimed, " That must be Pike's Peak!" If only the scarf of mist which turbaned its head would unroll and reveal the monarch's snowy crown!

"The Peak is like the Veiled Prophet of Khorassan," Cleopatra said; "it shrouds its head in mystery."

The comparison was more apt than she knew; for the veiled prophet was a hoary impostor, — not Pike's Peak, after all, but Cheyenne Mountain, which might indeed have won the enthusiasm of the girls for its own merits but for the overweening reputation of Captain Zebulon Pike's famous monument. Pike's Peak, when they did see it, dominated the landscape and dwarfed all rivals, its majestic summit towering above timber-line among snows and clouds to the height of 14,237 feet. How their desert-tired eyes revelled in the long sweeping lines, ranges rising above ranges and curling like the onward sweep of breakers ready to engulf the pretty town of Colorado Springs, where they now left the railroad!

Old travellers though they were, and Mrs. Morse fastidious to fault-finding, they all found "The Antlers" one of the most satisfactory hotels which they had ever visited.

"For once we have found a hotel with an appropriate name," said Mrs. Morse, as she enjoyed her antelope steak; and Madeleine added, —

"'What shall he have who kills the deer?
He shall have the head and the horns to wear.'"

After dinner they took a carriage and drove across the tawny *mesa*, or table-land, through the far-famed Garden of the Gods to Manitou. Madeleine found a resemblance in the drive to the Roman Campagna; the grotesquely shaped rocks reminded her of the remains of aqueducts and of other ruins. "The Gateway," as it is called, seemed like a castle of the mediæval period. As they threaded the park of strange natural monuments, their fancy ran riot among the fantastic forms which met their eye.

They drove first through Glen Eyrie, General Palmer's beautiful estate, named for the eagle's nests built long since upon jutting ledges

COLUMNS OF RED SANDSTONE.

of the cliff. Here columns of red sandstone had been worn into rude statuesque forms: an enormous whity-green griffin, a lion after the Assyrian type, and Lot's wife changed to sandstone instead of to salt, were some of the weird shapes. Nearer Manitou they passed a woman in white, a still better Lot's wife, and two gigantic giraffes or camels. Then followed such a zoölogical exhibition that Cleopatra suggested that some prehistoric Barnum had here been petrified. Then followed more of Nature's architecture, — the "Temple of Isis," with its strange towers and archways, and the "Cathedral Spires," which Madeleine thought as beautiful in its way as fair Melrose.

"SHE HAS LIVED IN LEADVILLE EVER SINCE IT WAS PROJECTED."

Shortly after they made their entry into Manitou, which they found to be a village of cottages and summer hotels, clinging like Swiss chalets to the slopes of a picturesque cañon. They drove past the showy bathhouse, various hotels, and private residences, — among the latter Grace Greenwood's cottage, — to their resting-place at the Iron Springs Hotel.

Mrs. Morse was astonished at the elegance and convenience of her surroundings. "I thought we were going to camp in the wilderness among savages, and just look at those people on the hotel piazza! They are just as civilized as anybody else. I had a chat with that lady with her dress cut in the heart-shaped style, and really I would not have known that she had not lived in New York all her life, and she says she has lived in Leadville ever since it was projected. Only fancy! Leadville! And yet she has managed to get up a very stylish coiffure. I thought every one wore their hair à la Cheyenne at Leadville."

A COLORADO SAVAGE.

"Dear mother, do speak a little lower!" whispered Madeleine. "I am afraid that young lady in the scarlet jacket has taken umbrage at what you have said."

"Why should she? She is a New-Yorker; any one can tell with half an eye that that's a Redfern jacket."

Mrs. Morse had spoken too loudly. A young man in foppish eye-glasses turned and remarked, "My sister's coat was made by a London tailor, but she is a Denver girl."

Mrs. Morse subsided into the house, too much mortified to apologize; but Cleopatra came to the rescue with a merry laugh. "Forgive our Eastern ignorance!" she exclaimed, extending her hand. "Believe me that we are filled with admiration as well as astonishment by all we see in this wonderful country."

No one could resist Cleopatra's engaging manners, and the young man asked permission to present his sister, Miss Hurlburt, of Idaho Springs. Mr. Hurlburt explained that he was in the mining business at Central City, just across the Mountain from Idaho Springs; and Cleopatra asked a number of intelligent questions, which showed that she was already somewhat acquainted with the subject.

"THAT A REDFERN JACKET."

"You are surely not an Eastern girl," Miss Hurlburt exclaimed, with genuine admiration; "at least not any farther east than Wichita."

"I am a genuine Western girl," Cleopatra replied; "I belong to the army. I was born at Fort Sill, and have rattled around to nearly every frontier post in the West. An ambulance is my natural home."

"How jolly!" exclaimed Miss Hurlburt; "but I am afraid of your friends, — they are New-Yorkers."

"They imagined you were from New York too and there is only one compliment higher than that which a New-Yorker can pay."

"And what is that, pray?"

"To think you are English."

Miss Hurlburt's nose took a higher elevation. "There are plenty of young English ranchmen out here, but we don't think anything of them. They are regular cowboys in their dress and manners really as bad as Buffalo Bill. The idea of being pleased at having any one think you English!" and Miss Hurlburt laughed merrily.

On the next day Madeleine, Cleopatra, Yulee, and the Hurlburts made the ascent of Pike's Peak on horseback, which they found to be a much longer ride than they anticipated. The hoary giant seemed to keep its place at the same relative distance, just at the head of the gorge, with provoking persistence. They rode for hours, and it looked very little nearer. "You have heard the story," said Mr. Hurlburt, "of two travellers in Colorado who had been frequently deceived in the matter of distance by our wonderful atmosphere. Having reached a very small brook, one of them took off his coat. 'What are you going to do?' asked the other. 'It looks as if I could step across,' replied the first, 'but I am not going to be fooled again; it may be a couple of miles for all I know, and I am going to be ready to swim."

THE LATEST ENGLISH STYLE.

Yulee had brought her botanists' can, and exclaimed from time to time at the mountain flowers, — the new species of columbine, and the Alpine flora which showed themselves as they mounted above timberline, the deep blue gentians, and the American Edelweiss. Mr. Hurlburt professed himself more interested in geology, and spoke of a fine collection which he wished to show her.

Then some one spoke of the Ute Pass, — the trail by which the Indians of this tribe were accustomed to file down the mountains to visit the mineral springs at Manitou, and of which they were very fond.

"It seems a pity," said Madeleine, "that they should be driven so far away from their favorite haunts."

"Colorado people do not see the pity," Mr. Hurlburt replied, with a laugh which was not altogether pleasant. "We would like nothing

A STREET IN LEADVILLE

better than to have every Indian cleared from the State, and we'll manage it too."

"What will become of them then?"

"I don't know. I am sure I don't care if they are all driven into the Pacific. We have had our share of them. It is very easy for Eastern people to be sentimental about the Indians. I would like to have the whole parcel of them shipped East, and dumped by instalments in the different cities."

Yulee made a quick telegraphic motion to Madeleine not to betray her, and that young lady replied: "I don't know but that would be a very good plan. They could not go on with their old savage life there, and the children would gradually become educated by the very force of their surroundings. I don't see but we have as much room for them amongst us as for the dynamiters, the lowest class of the negroes, the ignorant peasants of Europe, and the Chinese."

"The Chinese are not so bad," replied Mr. Hurlburt. "I am in favor of their being employed in the mines, and have stood by them through more than one riot. There is only one Indian for whom Colorado people have a thorough respect, and that was the Ute chief Ouray. He was without doubt the friend of the white man; he befriended and protected starving miners, even when they were prospecting on his land, and while he lived he did a great deal toward keeping his turbulent tribe in order. He had a neat house and an orchard of cherry and other fruit trees. After his death, when the tribe was moved, his widow Chipeta petitioned to remain in her home. But we did not want any Indians in that part of the State, and we sent her packing."

"Wasn't zat what you call razzer hard?" asked Yulee.

"Well, yes; but there doesn't seem to be any way of meeting the Indian except his own, — of cruelty and revenge."

Madeleine was silent. This man, who seemed just and clearheaded on every other subject. lost all idea of justice when he discussed the Indian problem; and she found this frequently the case in the West. She was obliged to admit that they had many arguments upon their side. Surely the Government, in making no efforts to civilize and educate the Indians, was doing a wrong to its white settlers by forcing them to live in dangerous proximity to savages. Mr. Hurlburt was right: there was no longer any room in America for savages; they *must* be either killed or civilized,— could Christian Americans hesitate as to which method should be employed?

Major Atchison arrived after a few days; but the acquaintance with the Hurlburts had now progressed so far that an invitation to visit the mines at Central City and to spend a few days at their home at Idaho Springs was extended and accepted. Denver was visited *en route*,— a great, enterprising city, with little to distinguish it from an Eastern city of the same size.

Central City was one of the first mining-regions opened, and was originally known as Pike's Peak. Letters directed simply to " Pike's Peak near Fort Laramie " found their owners here.

Up Clear Creek Cañon the train from Denver threaded its way past exhausted gulches where Chinamen still patiently wash for gold, up to the richer regions of the Black Hawk mines. The cañon was here so narrow that the houses seemed to cling desperately to the sides of the cliffs, and the roof of one was frequently the dooryard of another. Madeleine noticed that one family who had no yard of any description, a shelf in the cliff having been cut for their house, kept their cow upon the roof.

The mine with which Mr. Hurlburt was connected was called " the Bobtail." It was so named from the fact that in early times the ore was hauled out on a raw-hide by an old bob-tailed ox. Now a company of wealthy capitalists work the mine by means of complicated machinery. Five stories of galleries have been excavated; the lowest, eleven hundred feet below the surface, runs for hundreds of feet into the heart of the mountain.

The girls threaded one of these damp, dark passages for a mile or so, — a tunnel which had cost one hundred dollars per foot to cut, and which reminded Madeleine of the Catacombs, and Major Atchison of the galleries within the Rock of Gibraltar. Much trouble was experienced by the miners from meeting with springs of water while tracing a vein of ore, and a great part of the mine was flooded.

"Think of being lost in one of these underground chambers!" said Cleopatra with a shudder.

"It happened to me once," replied Mr. Hurlburt. "A part of the mine behind me caved in, and I was shut in with two of the men. We knew there was another way to the daylight, but our lanterns gave out and we wandered about for forty-eight hours trying to find the exit. We were rescued at last by Ah Lee, a Chinaman, whose life, I suppose, I saved when some of our miners had him at their mercy. He made up an exploring party of one, found us, and dragged us out when we had given up hope and lain down to die. So, you see, I believe in Chinamen."

AH LEE.

"Perhaps, if some one of Indian blood had saved your life, you would believe in Indians," said Madeleine.

"Perhaps; only I never had that experience," Mr. Hurlburt replied incredulously.

Out in the open air once more, they passed to the stamping-mill, and watched the crushing and washing of the ore by swift and powerful machinery. An air-drill was being tested near by, and the engineer in charge of the air-compressor wore a frightened expression. "When the pressure gets a little greater," he remarked, "I am going to light out; it'll take the side out of the house just as easy."

They stepped into the Bank, and while there a small "placer" miner brought in two great nuggets which the cashier reported worth eight hundred dollars, fifteen dollars to the ounce. In the Cyclops Assay Office a fine cabinet of specimens was shown them, and marvellous stories were told, until Cleopatra declared that the very water which she drank seemed gritty with gold.

"I understand," said Yulee, "why ze dentistry is not a good business here. You sall only to drink of ze water to fill of gold ze cavity of ze toof."

Mr. Hurlburt was greatly amused. The wit of this young Italian girl, as he considered her, greatly fascinated him.

The next day a dashing ride across the mountain took them to Idaho Springs.

What a drive it was! Up through the gathering mists, vainly hoping that they would roll away and disclose the view from the summit, — one of the grandest in all Colorado. They rested the horses occasionally to gather wild-flowers, — columbine, weigelia, harebells, and larkspur, — and to collect glittering specimens of rose quartz. Near the summit they passed a lonely cabin once occupied by a highwayman named Grab-em-all Jim.

And now the driver put on the brakes, and they ground and slid down the precipitous road, gullied by the rains into many a "thank-you-Ma'am," too narrow for a team to pass, with a ravine on the right hand and a rocky wall upon the left.

The girls clutched frantically to their seats; but Mr. Hurlburt, used to rough riding, grumbled: "Don't put on the brakes, driver; let the horses run! I've heard Bill Updyke took General Grant and Mrs. Sartoris down the mountain in ten minutes. Can't you beat that record?"

The driver mutttered to himself that a fast fool broke his neck here the other day trying to do it; but Mr. Hurlburt replied: "He was drunk. No danger at all if a man knows how to drive! Perhaps you had better let me take the reins."

A DANGEROUS RIDE.

The driver loosens the brakes with a dogged, " I kin drive as fast as the next one if you will take the risk."

Thenceforth the girls close their eyes and wish themselves in the following vehicle with Mrs. Morse, Yulee, and the Major; while Cleopatra murmurs, " Oh! would it not have been better if that air-drill had exploded while we were looking at it yesterday ? "

Presently the carriages swept triumphantly into the pretty village of Idaho Springs. Here Miss Hurlburt greeted them on the piazza of a Queen Anne cottage; and after a supper of delicious brook-trout they were taken to see the soda springs, the great swimming-bath, and other sights of the town.

A week was spent very pleasantly with their new friends, and then the entire party turned their faces once more westward; for both Miss Hurlburt and her brother had decided that they would join them for a month's camping in the National Park.

CHAPTER XII.

THE ROCKIES AND SALT LAKE.

NOTWITHSTANDING their delightful experiences, it was plainly to be seen that something was the matter with the Major. He had been depressed ever since the arrival of an official letter marked "War Department." Cleopatra, who was used to her father's moods, knew that he was blue, and used her merriest wiles to beguile him. It was of no avail; the good man became gloomier and gloomier.

"You have changed so, Pat," he said to her one day. "You used to be the maddest little romp in the West. Little Hurlburt here couldn't hold a candle to you for pranks and mischief, but Vassar has toned you down so that I scarcely know you."

"Don't you like me so, father?" Cleopatra asked, much troubled.

"Like you! You have vastly improved; but will you like the West now? You are a cultivated young lady, fitted for the best there is in the East. I'm afraid our military posts will seem a little — Well, I fancy you'll call us *crude* now."

Cleopatra laughed, and hugged her father. "You know I adore the West," she said. "Nothing could induce me to live anywhere else. I love dear romantic old Santa Fé, with its fascinating Spanish history. I am going to study it up when we get there, and I intend

CAÑON OF THE ARKANSAS.

to coax the Bishop to let me read all the records of the Franciscan friars who discovered the country, and perhaps I shall find some of the state papers of the old Spanish Governors, which were sold for waste-paper."

The Major groaned. "Do not set your heart too much on Santa Fé. An army officer's life is as uncertain as that of a Methodist minister's; you know they say their chickens always lie down and turn up their feet to be tied whenever a covered wagon passes by."

Cleopatra whistled. "Oh, that's it!" she said; "we are going to be transferred. Well, we have enjoyed the luxury of a peaceable post long enough, I suppose. I think I should like a little campaigning. It would be ever so exciting and nice to chase the Apaches into Mexico. I always liked the Indians, and I want to see more of them; the wilder the better. Do tell me that we are going among the hostiles."

"There are no hostiles now," said the Major. "No; there is no probability of my being ordered into active service, and if I were I should not take you." And after this the Major vouchsafed nothing further. Cleopatra knew that it would be of no use to question him, but that in his own time all would be explained.

The party now dashed through some of the most magnificent scenery in the world; for the adventurous Denver and Rio Grande Railroad climbs and tunnels, zigzags, plunges, coasts, or creeps wherever the most sublime scenery of Colorado is to be found. No difficulties have been too great, no natural barriers insurmountable. It would seem that the enterprising managers of this road had sent it in search of every stupendous cañon and every mountain peak of unusual grandeur.

Their first genuine surprise was in the cañon of the Arkansas. Here they were filled with what Ruskin calls the deep and pure emotion of astonishment. The Arkansas River, foaming over its rocky bed, chafes its way at the bottom of this awful ravine, in some places shut in closely by two perpendicular walls of basaltic rock so high that from the bottom the sky seemed a ribbon of blue. Along this prisoned river-bed the railroad is laid, — beside it, where there is room for the two to divide the narrow gallery; over it, by means of bridges and flying buttresses, where the river fills the floor of the gorge. It was a magnificent achievement in engineering, and was so appreciated by them all. But there was another part of the route which struck them as more truly stupendous and sublime. This was the Black Cañon, a longer ravine, the sides rising to grander heights, — at one point more than three thousand feet in a nearly perpendicular wall.

They made the trip by moonlight, on an "observation car" without roof. The girls were closely wrapped in shawls and blankets; for though it was an August night, the air was very cold. The roaring of the train was reverberated from the rocky walls, giving the impression that another must be approaching at the same dizzy speed and that a collision was inevitable. Every now and then the chasm wound or turned abruptly, so that it seemed as if the engine were about to plunge straight against a solid wall of rock. By their side the Gunnison River dashed jetty black, but flecked with white foam. Now a cascade sprang from a cliff and was blown into a veil of mist before reaching the bottom, and now they rounded the Currecanti Needle, — a beautiful cone-shaped pinnacle where it is said the Utes once lighted signal-fires. Down the still narrower ravine of the Cimarron, and then with a shriek from the whistle they dashed out of this valley of enchantment.

Yulee was profoundly impressed; these were the first mountains which she had seen. Even Madeleine, who was familiar with the Alps, was surprised. "I did not know that we had anything like this in America," she exclaimed, and was quite out of patience with a geologist who had been introduced to them, who persisted in telling her that this was the finest region in the world for auriferous pyrites (gold ore), galena (silver ore), tourmaline, microline, wavellite, and magnetite. He was attracted by the beauty of an opal which Mrs. Morse wore, but surprised that lady by calling it a fine specimen of hydrated silica.

Yulee noticed the look of annoyance on Madeleine's face. "And yet," she explained to Mr. Hurlburt, "see sall be fery fond of geology; but it ees not ze time to talk of zat when ze soul is touch by ze grand. It ees as if one should tell me what ze good God sall look like."

MISS HURLBURT.

Mr. Hurlburt, who was intensely practical, tried to argue that science never detracted from sublimity. "When Ruskin tells me," he said, "that 'mountains are to the body of the earth what violent muscular action is to the body of man,' and that 'the muscles and tendons of its anatomy are in the mountains brought out with fierce and convulsive energy, full of expression, passion, and strength,' then I maintain that he asserts a purely scientific fact, but in doing so he makes the mountains seem more poetic to me than before."

Yulee shrugged her shoulders in the pretty way which she inherited from her mother. "I sink zat Mr. Rus — Rus (how you call him?) more of poet as geologist," she said.

Mr Hurlburt laughed. He was fast becoming very much interested in Yulee. Madeleine saw it and was displeased. She thought that Yulee ought to be conscious of his admiration, and that she was not acting fairly to Captain Saunters.

Miss Hurlburt saw her brother's admiration also, and, like the good sister she was, aided and abetted him at every turn by engaging the others in sprightly conversation and leading them away to see fictitious points of interest whenever the party left the cars. She looked like an *ingénue*, this fair-haired young girl, but she was

THE COWBOY.

THE MINISTER.

THE SENATOR.

as deep a schemer as a Wall Street broker, and as clever a manipulator of the matrimonial market for others as for herself. Personally she had refused three army officers, a half dozen young ranchmen and miners, two tourists from the East who had each known her just forty-eight hours, all of the unmarried ministers of her acquaintance, and one Senator. She had given the Senator consideration for the space of three quarters of an hour, for she was not without ambition; but like most Western girls she was true and good at heart, and when the Senator returned to ascertain the result of her deliberation, he stood with arms akimbo, a disgusted and much astonished man.

A little before the train reached Marshall Pass, on the crest of the continent, — the great "divide" which decides whether a rain-drop shall finally flow into the Atlantic or the Pacific, — there was a halt made at some long snow-sheds which protect the track from the winter avalanches, and the passengers all alighted.

THE ROCKIES AND SALT LAKE.   171

Miss Hurlburt suggested that they should all scramble up the side of the mountain a little way to some patches of snow which gleamed white in the sunshine, though aspens were shivering beside

"LONG SNOW-SHEDS WHICH PROTECT THE TRACK."

them, and there indulge in an August snowball frolic. Cleopatra followed enthusiastically; her father and Madeleine more slowly. Mrs. Morse looked on with amused interest, but Mr. Hurlburt drew

Yulee's attention to some lupines growing almost out of another snowbank a little way down the gorge. What womanly intuition was it which told Miss Hurlburt that her brother and Yulee would be seized with a botanical craze to examine these flowers? Nothing could have been more unconscious than the extremely general way in which she invited *all* in the other direction, and yet the little minx knew just how many would accept her invitation.

Marshall Pass is above timber-line, among clouds and snow; but after leaving the Pass the track begins to descend the Pacific by a series of long inclined planes, — " coasts." Cleopatra called them, — of the dizzy grade of two hundred and twenty feet to the mile.

Soon after they were flying over the Great American Desert, tawny brown in color, with crumbling sand-hills, or "buttes," shutting in the view. Madeleine noticed that Yulee was graver than usual, that she no longer sparkled in repartee with Mr. Hurlburt, but occupied herself in quietly reading, or more often in looking dreamily from the window, book in hand, but her gaze apparently absorbed by the troops of wild sun-flowers which seemed to keep pace with the flying train. They struck against the car windows like saucy forward creatures demanding attention.

Madeleine was glad to see her more quiet and thoughtful. " She is coming to her senses," she thought, "and remembers what she owes the Captain." Madeleine forgot for the moment that Yulee was quite unconscious that she owed Captain Saunters anything; and as the romance which Madeleine had woven between them existed only in that young lady's imagination, the gallant Captain had at this time no part in her thoughts.

Their next stop after this was at Salt Lake City. Here all the party were rendered indignant by what they saw.

" It is almost enough to make me ashamed of my uniform," said the Major, " to think that our Government tolerates such infamy and treason; for open disobedience to its laws is nothing less."

They attended service in the "Tabernacle,"—a building shaped like an inverted boat,—and the girls could scarcely contain their wrath and quietly sit through the sermon.

"I did not realize that such things existed in our own land," said Madeleine. "I knew that away in Turkey there are harems, and that several wives are permitted by the Mohammedan religion

THE MORMON TABERNACLE.

to one man; but I confess I never understood until now that such indignity to women was permitted in our own Christian country. Why do not the people of the United States rise up *en masse*, and say that such things shall not be?"

"The people of the United States know very little, and care less about it," said Mr. Hurlburt; "that is the boast of the Mormons. They have taken possession of this garden of the Lord, isolated from civilization by the desert. They have until the recent building of the railroad conducted themselves as they pleased, beyond the reach, and almost beyond the knowledge, of the rest of the world."

"But Government must know how they are spreading,—that they have colonies in five States and Territories. Their converts are pouring into New York, three hundred on a single steamship. Why does not Government put a stop to such emigration?"

"In the first place Government is an extremely impersonal individual, and the Mormon body is very rich. I am afraid Government's conscience is easily put to sleep with Mormon soothing-syrup," said Mr. Hurlburt. "It is, however, an alarming thing to consider that in my own State of Colorado, where the Republican and the Democratic vote are nearly balanced, the Mormon population is large enough to give the majority to either party."

"I don't care a penny for the political aspect of the question," said Cleopatra, excitedly. "What I cannot understand is how any woman can submit to such personal and social degradation. How I wish I could talk to the girls here! I would like nothing better than to set up a school in this place."

"You would be boycotted for your pains," said Mr. Hurlburt. "There is a large Gentile population here now, but they do not mingle with the Mormons. By the way, speaking of the term by which the Mormons politely designate the rest of the world, it is a curious fact that most of the '*Gentiles*' here are *Jews*."

"I am glad to see them here; for I am sure, strange as it may sound, that their example will have a Christianizing effect. I am glad, too, to see the Roman Catholic Cross over so many buildings, and especially to see that they have a seminary for girls here. The ascetic example of the nuns is a beautiful contrast to the grossness about them. I saw a sweet, little, flaxen-haired Swedish girl yesterday morning, as we rode out to the lake. She was sitting under one of the few large trees on the way, feeding some doves. She looked so innocent and happy that I could not bear to think of her growing up in this dreadful place."

"I think," said Madeleine, "that when these girls see that other women insist on having one undivided husband to themselves alone, they will want the same or none. Do the men never genuinely fall in love here, I wonder! One might do a real missionary work here by distributing the better class of novels. A pure, sweet love-story would, it seems to me, rouse nobler ideals."

"But did you notice the young men at the Tabernacle?" asked Cleopatra. "I did not notice one that would figure as the hero of a romance. I have only seen one Latter-Day Saint reading an Eastern newspaper since we came, and he seemed to be having a hard time to puzzle it out. And one sees no nice-looking boys, such as we might imagine were attending high school or preparing for college, or such manly fellows as we saw in the Kansas farming districts. But if the girls could be educated, they would see for themselves how much better the loneliest life would be than such companionship."

LITTLE SWEDISH GIRL.

The next day the party made an excursion by rail to the Great Salt Lake, — a lovely inland sea with mountains in the distance, reminding Madeleine strongly of Lake Geneva. The gentlemen bathed in the water, and found it buoyant and easy to swim in.

Cleopatra amused herself by photographing the people who frequented the pavilion. She had already secured views of some of the homes of the settlers as well as of the grand scenery through which they had passed.

On their return they took carriages and drove about the city. They were shown the Lion House, the former residence of Brigham Young, the Bee-Hive or Harem, the Endowment House, and the great unfinished Temple. They were amused by such signs as "Zion Co-operative Store," and "Holiness to the Lord Groceries," and the like. From the city they drove to the neglected Mormon Cemetery. A more desolate abode of the dead can scarcely be imagined. Madeleine called it "lonely," but Yulee said this was hardly the proper term. "I cannot imagine to myself," she said, "zat so many womens should be lonely togezzer." They read on one stone the names of the wives of George A. Smith, — " Bathsheba W., Lucy M., Zilpah S., Hannah M., Nancy G., Sarah A., Susan E."

A LATTER-DAY SAINT.

Some friends of the Major's invited the party to dinner at Camp Douglass, the pretty military post which overlooks Salt Lake City. Here they drew a long breath, for it seemed to them that they breathed a different atmosphere. The officers' houses were of neat brown-stone, and the parade-ground was set with Balm-of-Gilead trees. The interiors of the homes were furnished with all the tastefulness and elegance which officers' wives know so well how to evolve from furnishings which can be shut up in small compass at a moment's notice. Photographs of dear ones far away decorated the wall side by side with gun-racks and Indian curiosities, German favors, engravings from the "London Graphic," Japanese decorations, souvenirs of West Point or home, and many another pretty object which had been folded close and had travelled by ambulance from one part of the Union to another.

"I wish you could be stationed here, father," said Cleopatra; "then I should know what my duty in life was. I would make the acquaintance of some of these Mormon girls, — that little yellow-haired Swede, first of all."

A PIONEER'S HOME.

The Major gave a sudden start. "How did you find it out?" he asked.

"Find what out?" Cleopatra replied, much bewildered.

"I am transferred to Camp Douglass, ordered to report here a month from this date. Salt Lake will be our home for the present."

"Delightful!" exclaimed Cleopatra.

"'Delightful!' and here I have been dreading to tell you that it was necessary for us to come to such a God-forsaken place. I fancied you would take it hard, and I did not blame you. Well, girls are the most inexplicable creatures. The longer I lived with your mother the less I understood her. Your sister Barbara was a puzzle past finding out, and you are an enigma which I give up entirely."

"No, father," Cleopatra replied, radiantly happy; "you shall never give me up. I am going to be the most useful, the most delightful old maid that ever was, and you shall bless the day that I was ever born."

CHAPTER XIII.

CAMPING ON THE YELLOWSTONE.

AT Salt Lake City the party provisioned for their camping in the National Park, supplying their Commissary Department with an outfit of canned goods, — beef, tongue, Boston baked beans, oysters, condensed milk, sardines, canned fruits of various kinds, — crackers, bacon, coffee, and tea. They then proceeded by rail to Ogden, and from thence by the Utah Northern Railroad to Beaver Cañon, and across a range of mountains to the western entrance of the Park. This wonder-land of the genii is a tract of land, sixty-five miles north and south by fifty-five east and west, set apart from settlement by the Government as a pleasure-ground, and is situated in the northwestern corner of Wyoming Territory. Not far away is the Big Horn River, where Custer and his command met their death. Our party knew that they were to see great natural curiosities, and had heard of the marvellous hot springs and falls, but still were not prepared for the stupendous cañon and the awful geysers.

Not far from the railroad terminus they secured the services of an expert guide who furnished saddle-horses, mules, and spring-wagons, with camp equipage. His home and his Indian wife and children were objects of great interest to the girls. It seemed to all that Dick had met his wife more than half-way, going farther toward savagery than she had toward civilization.

"That is always the way of it," said Mr. Hurlburt. "I have known several white men who married Indian wives. They either regretted the experiment or relapsed to barbarism themselves. Nothing could induce me to make such a fool of myself."

Madeleine noticed that Yulee was silent, but that her look was no longer one of roguish merriment, but rather of pained confusion. She grew more and more indignant with the girl. "I wonder," she

DICK AND HIS FAMILY.

thought, "whether her braving the yellow fever for my sake was only a low kind of physical courage, and whether she lacks, after all, a high moral courage, or a nice perception between right and wrong."

They stopped, the first night of their expedition after leaving the railroad, at Marshall's Hotel; but the second they made their own camp, very much like the one in the pine-barrens of Florida. Their first objective point was the Madison River, or, as it is called here, the Fire Hole River. They visited only the Upper Geyser Basin; and all declared that it was the most wonderful day of their lives. "I had

CRATER OF "OLD FAITHFUL."

always thought," said Madeleine, "that the geysers would be like the fountains at Versailles on a day *des grands eaux!* I had no idea that they were so immense."

The Excelsior, whose eruption they did not see, spouts to a height of three hundred feet. They were delighted with the paint pools, orange, ruby, and rose-color, and especially with the Morning-glory Pool, which Mrs. Alice Wellington Rollins describes so exquisitely: " It is precisely like a morning-glory flower. Its long and slender throat, like the tube of the blossom, reaching from unknown depths below, branches out in ever-widening snowy walls, forming at last a perfectly symmetrical and exquisite chalice, which is filled with water of the loveliest robin's-egg blue. The rim of the chalice is delicately and regularly scalloped, and is edged with a tiny line of coral."

The greatest sensation of the day occurred near Old Faithful, which stands at the head of the valley, and is so named from its regular intervals of spouting, a little more than an hour apart. It began with a sputter, then a quick fusillade of jets, increasing in height to over a hundred feet, and then dying away in steam. When they first arrived the crater had an innocent extinct look, and Yulee wandered quite near to examine the encrustations of silica with which it was bordered. It began to boil, and she drew back to only a short distance, watching the rapidly growing fountains, not hearing, in the noise of the geyser, the call of the guide, and would undoubtedly have been scalded, had not Mr. Hurlburt suddenly caught her away. He was very pale, and when they stood breathless just out of reach of that thunderous descending column of water and spray, an expression of unmistakable emotion came into his face — an intense thankfulness born of equal dismay — which told of a man's deepest affection. For an instant the look was answered in Yulee's mirror-like eyes; then the others crowded around with exclamations and warnings. Not a word had been said, and yet these two young people knew that each loved the other.

THE GEYSER LAND.

All day the party wandered through the enchanted valley, visiting geyser after geyser. The Giant proved to be a huge horn-shaped

THE GROTTO.

crater five feet across. The guide told them that this geyser spouted to the height of one hundred and thirty feet. They waited for it an hour or so, but the genius within was sullen and refused to come forth. Many of the springs were of a deep blue color, containing sulphate of copper, and held in beautiful porcelain-lined basins. Following down the river, they passed other smaller geysers with odd names, — the Black Sand, the Bath-Tub, the Punch-Bowl, and the Pyramid. Some of these were in eruption, and others at rest. But the most beautiful spectacle of the day, all agreed, was the Grotto. This was a fanciful formation, resembling a ruined palace with arches and carvings of mimic architecture. Profiting by Yulee's experience at Old Faithful, all kept at a respectful distance from the Grotto, though Cleopatra longed to explore it. Mr. Hurlburt focussed her camera and waited patiently, and was rewarded by a beautiful display; the jets, as they issued from different openings, from her point of view grouped themselves in a superb fan sixty feet high.

After leaving this spot, strolling about in search of brilliantly colored encrustations, Madeleine found herself for a little while alone with Yulee. It was an opportunity not to be lost. "Yulee," she asked gently, "do you realize that Mr. Hurlburt is interested in you?"

A deep crimson burned on the girl's cheek, but she answered frankly, "I haf sometime think so. It is possible I do deceive myself."

"Would it not be worse to deceive him? Do you think it is right to let him go on loving you when you know that your marriage is impossible, if for no other reason, from his prejudice toward the Indians?"

"You have right; he should know I was Indian."

"Then why don't you tell him?"

"That should be very hard. I would razzer you to do it."

"Then shall I tell him all?"

She darted a quick appreciative glance. "I would make you many sanks."

There was no opportunity for such confidences that day or evening, and the next day the party drove over the mountain "divide" which separates the streams which flow into the Missouri from those which seek the Columbia, to the Hot Springs on the south-

"YULEE AND MADELEINE WERE BOTH FOND OF FISHING."

west arm of Yellowstone Lake. The lake is twenty-two miles in length, and from ten to fifteen in width. From their camp they commanded a beautiful view of the lake, which was of an exquisite blue shading into tourmaline-green. The springs bubble up inside of funnel-shaped craters which extend into the very lake, so that at this point the fisher can catch his trout, and with a whisk of his rod drop them into the boiling spring and cook them without removing them from his hook. Yulee and Madeleine were both fond of fishing, and had many a fine catch during this expedition.

The next day they proceeded along the western shore of the lake, past some curious mud volcanoes, to the Yellowstone River. It was one of the aims of the Government, in setting apart the Park, to make it a refuge for the larger wild animals, which are being rapidly exterminated. In some mysterious way these intelligent animals have learned that they are safe here. The guide said he had often shot elk here before the game laws were enacted, and told of one day when five deer had rewarded a hunt. " There was a gentleman made his way into the Park last winter," he said, " who saw a herd of a hundred and twenty elk feeding about here. He says that at first they were quite tame, but he gave one loud 'Whoopee!' and stampeded the whole herd. It must have been a lovely sight; but I'm afeard my old rifle would have accidentally fired itself about that time." The guide promised to secure them a pair of antlers, procured in accordance with Government regulations. They saw wild fowl frequently, while on the margin of the lake, and met a party who had seen buffalo.

While descending the river, Madeleine, who was riding, managed to secure Mr. Hurlburt as an escort, Yulee having decided that for that morning she preferred the wagon with Mrs. Morse. It was easy to lead Mr. Hurlburt to converse about Yulee. When not talking to her he was continually speaking of her, and Madeleine told him that Yulee had desired her to tell him of her parentage, hoping that the knowledge would not forfeit her his friendship, since it was certainly no fault of hers.

" I am aware," said Mr. Hurlburt, " that Miss Ponce is a Minorcan, and that the race is not highly considered in Florida, where they were once treated almost as slaves; but the name Ponce is one of the noblest in Spanish history, and I have no doubt that we can trace her family back to ancestors of whom any one might be proud."

Madeleine was really sorry for the enthusiastic young man, for she knew that what she was about to say would be most painful; but she went on with the calm decision of a practised surgeon. "On her mother's side, Yulee may descend, as you say, from some haughty family, but her father was an obscure man who took his wife's name because he had none of his own."

A CASCADE IN THE YELLOWSTONE PARK.

"No matter how obscure, provided there was no crime to hide; and even if that were the case, I am sure that no ancestral taint can have descended to Yulee. Whatever her father was, she is not responsible for him."

"Would you feel so if I were to tell you that he was an Indian?"

The young man started; evidently he had not expected this, and the blow was terrible.

"Impossible!" he exclaimed.

"He is a Seminole, but civilized, and in some respects a remarkable man."

The shock was only momentary, and the sterling metal in the young man's nature now showed itself. "I am free to confess, Miss Morse," he said, "that what you tell me is a great surprise to me, and that I am sorry for it; but I hold to what I said.

Yulee cannot help it: it is no fault of hers, and I don't mind telling you that I love her, and mean to ask her to become my wife."

Madeleine was both pleased and pained. She had expected to see him relinquish all pretensions to Yulee, and had fully prepared herself to despise him. She was surprised to find him equal to the test, and she admired his manliness.

"Then, Mr. Hurlburt," she said, "I have a still more painful task: I must tell you that there is some one else, — a noble, grand man who is educating Yulee in the expectation that she will marry him by-and-by, — a man who is as attractive as he is generous, and who is in every way worthy of her."

The whole attitude of the young man changed from that of a conqueror, one who had overcome his baser nature and deserved the prize he coveted, to that of a defeated and broken man.

He gave one great sob, which some way did not sound unmanly to Madeleine. "I might have known that there would be some one else," he said. "A girl like Yulee does n't grow up to such loveliness without plenty of people finding it out." Then he straightened himself in his saddle and extended his hand. "I thank you," he said: "you've meant to do the square thing by me, I know."

And Madeleine, conscious that she had meant to do right, — more than this, sure that she had done so, — wrung the hand held toward her, much to the mystification of Miss Hurlburt, who just then came into view.

Others might have observed the sudden gloom which had fallen upon these two young people, had they not reached very shortly after this episode the culminating point of their tour, the object for which it had been made, — the Falls of the Yellowstone. There are two of these cascades, not more than a quarter of a mile apart. The Upper Falls seemed to them very beautiful, but when they reached the lower ones their enthusiasm knew no bounds.

Professor Hayden, who first thoroughly explored this region, has best described it. He says: "No language can do justice to the wonderful grandeur and beauty of the cañon below the Lower Falls. Standing near the margin of the Lower Falls and looking down the cañon, which looks like an immense chasm or cleft in the basalt, with its sides twelve hundred to fifteen hundred feet high, and decorated with the most brilliant colors that the human eye ever saw, with the rocks weathered into an unlimited variety of forms, with here and there a pine sending its roots into the clefts on the sides, as if struggling with a sort of uncertain success to maintain an existence, the whole presents a picture that it would be difficult to surpass in Nature. After the waters of the Yellowstone roll over the upper descent, they flow with great rapidity over the apparently flat rocky bottom, which spreads out to nearly double its width above the Falls, and continues thus until near the Lower Falls, when the channel again contracts, and the waters seem, as it were, to gather themselves into one compact mass, and plunge over the descent of three hundred and fifty feet in detached drops of foam as white as snow; some of the large globules of water shoot down like the contents of an exploded rocket. It is a sight far more beautiful, though not so grand or impressive as that of Niagara Falls."

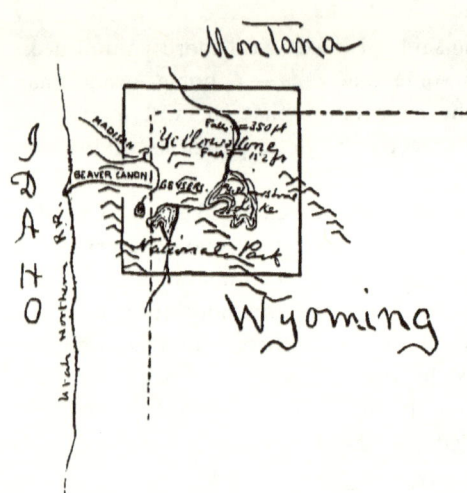

It was near the Lower Cascade that Madeleine gave Yulee a partial report of her embassy.

' And you did tell zat I sall be Indian?"

"Yes, Yulee; and oh! I was so sorry for him, for he really seemed devoted to you."

"Devote, — I know not what you mean by zat. You say he haf give me up?"

"Yes, Yulee; but he said it was no fault of yours, and I am sure it was a great trial to him. He loved you, Yulee, and he takes it very hard."

Yulee looked incredulous, slightly scornful even. She could not understand the love which gave her up for no fault of hers. As for Madeleine, no one ever did mischief with kinder intent. She was inflicting pain upon friends and bringing doubt and misunderstanding between two loving hearts, one of whom had showed for her the greatest devotion, even to the risking of life itself; and all because she mistakenly fancied that Yulee was pledged to Captain Saunters. The trouble which she was bringing upon Yulee was reflected in her own heart. The loyalty with which she labored for what she supposed were the Captain's interests was proof of a deeper interest in him than she would acknowledge to herself. She took a stern pleasure in helping on this marriage, telling herself that the dumb revolt which she sometimes felt towards it was only because Yulee seemed hardly to appreciate her happiness.

Their tour in the Park was now at an end. A few days more of rather disconsolate riding and nights of camping brought them round to their outfitting point. A gloom seemed to have fallen on the party. Miss Hurlburt instantly perceived her brother's unhappiness, and sprang to the conclusion that Yulee had rejected him. Indignant and surprised, she visited her resentment upon the unhappy girl by a distant and freezing manner, very different from the sisterly effusion with which she had hitherto deluged her. Madeleine was troubled and silent. Cleopatra felt the fall in the social thermometer without knowing the cause, and did her best — as during her father's depression — by quips and pranks to keep up the spirits of the party.

"You are a real life-preserver, Pat, dear," Madeleine said; "without you we would sink in the Dead Sea of Despair."

IN THE GRAND CAÑON.

"A merry heart doeth good like a medicine," quoted Mrs. Morse. Cleopatra applied herself to the entertainment of Mr. Hurlburt, speaking of the temperance movement among the Black Hawk miners, in which she knew he was interested; but that young man was too deeply hurt to converse at all. He left Cleopatra abruptly, when she was in the midst of an account of how she had carried the pledge through her father's command, and had started a temperance society which had accomplished much good.

"Excuse me to your friend," he said to Madeleine later, "but I do not feel as if I could ever talk to a woman again. It is well that our trip is over, and that we part to-morrow at Ogden, and that my sister and I return to Colorado. I cannot bear to be with you any longer."

His leave-taking from Yulee was of the most commonplace order. How could it be otherwise, as they stood in the station before the entire party?

"I wish you a pleasant trip," he said, with a tragic and desperate expression of countenance.

Yulee's lip quivered. "I haf much to sank you for ze flowers of Colorado," she said with dignity.

Then Miss Hurlburt grasped her brother's arm, saying, "Edward, we shall lose the train;" and they were gone.

Cleopatra looked on, much amused, and remarked to Madeleine: —

"'I remember the day that we met,
The way and the day that we parted ;
You vowed you could never forget,
And I feared we were both broken-hearted '

And I presume to say it will end in the same way, — they will have forgotten each other's names in less than ten years from now."

"I hope so," Madeleine replied dubiously; "but no, Pat, I'm afraid that Mr. Hurlburt at least is very much in earnest."

CHAPTER XIV.

CALIFORNIA AND ARIZONA.

AND now they rattled on over the Central Pacific Railroad through Nevada to California, which they found, in contrast to the frosty nights on the Yellowstone, verified its Spanish name of "hot furnace." They spent several days in San Francisco, visiting the Golden Gate Park, the Cliff House and Seal Rocks, Oakland, the Chinese quarter, and other points of interest, and then whisked away to the Yosemite, which they explored in connection with the Mariposa great trees.

The party spent the night at Clark's Ranch, and on the following morning rode to the Mariposa groves, a distance of only four miles. In the upper grove seven *Sequoia gigantea* were pointed out as having a circumference of over eighty feet. The largest tree in the lower grove is Grizzly Giant, which has a girth of ninety-three feet.

The next day they started by stage for the Yosemite Valley. It would take too long to describe in detail their wanderings here, as no incident bearing particularly on the future of the three girls, which was being decided by this trip, occurred in this beautiful spot. The view which Cleopatra decided to be her favorite one was that of the Sentinel, — a mountain of granite, of which it has been said, "Sentinel Rock combines more of picturesqueness and grandeur, perhaps, than any other rock-mass in the valley, its obelisk-like top reaching a

THE YOSEMITE VALLEY.

height of over three thousand feet, the face wall being almost vertical."

The Grand Cascade was not at its best, for the heat of summer had dwindled its fair proportions, and it is grandest in the spring when the snows begin to melt. "At such times the Yosemite Fall is described as grand beyond all power of expression. The summit of the upper fall is a little over twenty-six hundred feet above the valley; for fifteen hundred feet the descent is absolutely vertical and the rock is like a wall of masonry. Before this the fall of water sways and sweeps, yielding to the force of the fitful wind with a marvellous grace and endless variety of motion. For a moment it descends with continuous roar; in another instant it is caught, and, reversing its flight, rises upward in wreathing eddying mists, finally fading out like a summer cloud."

ONE OF THE BIG TREES.

Yulee's favorite spot was tranquil Mirror Lake, which so marvellously repeats its surrounding scenery, — the foliage, the mountains, the very clouds, — all so perfectly reflected that, as Yulee expressed it, "It is as if you sall float between two worlds."

Mr. James D. Smillie, of New York, famous as an artist and etcher, has exquisitely illustrated this charming spot. Madeleine was familiar with his pictures, and again and again exclaimed with delight as some new scene seemed like an old friend through their interpretation. "His name ought to be as closely connected with the Yosemite as Thomas Moran's is with the Yellowstone," she said, as they stood before the tremulous beauty of the Bridal Veil.

"I always connect Bierstadt with the Yosemite," said the Major.

"He is best known," replied Madeleine; "and it is a delightful thing that so many of our American artists have been made famous by American scenes. Surely there is enough that is picturesque in this glorious continent to occupy our artists at home. What are castles and stupid peasants to this?"

Cleopatra smiled as she thought how her friend's opinion had changed since a certain day at Vassar; but she forebore one of a woman's dearest delights, — that of saying, "I told you so."

They reached Los Angeles, the City of the Angels, at the height of the fruit season. Never before had they seen such a profusion of grapes, like Aladdin's gem fruit, — from the purple Mission to the topaz Muscat and pale Malaga, — such huge pears, peaches which did not have a flannelly taste, and such immense watermelons bursting with their own crumpy lusciousness. Los Angeles is now a city of fifty thousand inhabitants, with lovely suburban residences approached by avenues of palm and surrounded with orange-groves. They made a brief excursion to Santa Monica, its little watering-place on the Pacific, where they indulged in the luxury of surf-bathing, and saw heliotropes ten feet high and scarlet geraniums clambering to second-story windows.

It was hard to bid farewell to such a paradise; but it was time now to turn their faces eastward, and they were soon whizzing over the Atlantic and Pacific Railroad through Arizona, which Cleopatra was sure was so named because it *is* an arid zone, ah! But here, as everywhere else, there were signs of enterprise and progress. While dining at one of the stations, where they were served with every luxury of

TRANQUIL MIRROR LAKE.

an Eastern hotel, the Major remarked, " I can remember the time when the only 'hotel' in this place was kept by a Hibernian landlady who might have been the original of Cooper's —

> 'Good Mother Flanagan,
> Come fill the can again ;
> For you can fill. and we can swill,
> Good Mother Flanagan !'

"MOTHER FLANAGAN."

Only half of the description would apply to her, however; for though she could fill, the veriest toper would have found it hard to swallow the vile mixture which she dispensed."

The younger and more adventurous spirits were anxious to stop at Peach Springs and visit the Grand Cañon of the Colorado; but Mrs. Morse was a little weary, and it was feared that the journey might be too fatiguing for her.

" I am sure we have seen cañons enough dears," she said, feebly, " and it can't be finer than the Cañon of the Yellowstone."

" Listen to what the guide-book says," replied Madeleine. " There are Americans who saw Rome before they saw Niagara, who saw Mont Blanc before they saw the Yosemite, and who saw the Alps and the Pyrenees before they saw the Rockies and the Sierras. Let them have seen all these, with the Urals, the Andes, and the Himalayas thrown in; let them have seen the boiling geyser of Iceland and the belching craters of Ætna and Chimborazo; let them have looked upon the wonders of the Yellowstone and listened to the roar of Niagara; let them have traversed all the rest of the world, and until they have seen the Grand Cañon of the Colorado, the world's greatest wonder yet awaits them. Imagine a zigzag cañon three hundred miles long, perpendicular walls on either side of the river,

GRAND CAÑON, LOOKING EAST.

five thousand to six thousand feet in the air. Think of it! More than a mile of rock towering above you!"

Mrs. Morse looked frightened. " I would rather not think of it, Madeleine dear; and as for anything under heaven resembling all those different places at once, I cannot conceive of it."

Madeleine patiently explained that the cañon was not asserted to resemble, but to surpass in grandeur, all these localities; but Mrs. Morse was not attracted. She was better pleased with the desire of Major Atchison to stop at Fort Wingate and visit some old army friends, for she had an admiration for everything of a military nature.

Cleopatra was now in her element. Her spirits rose the moment she caught sight of the ambulances waiting for them at the station, and it needed strong self-control to keep her from embracing the orderly who saluted so respectfully.

At Fort Wingate Cleopatra met a number of ladies whom she had known; and the party were most hospitably entertained, as is always the case among army people. As the girls strolled out upon one of the pleasant verandas that evening, they caught each other's hands in pleased surprise. A well-built soldierly figure was crossing the parade-ground. "Of all persons in the world, — Captain Saunters!"

The Captain was as much surprised as they, and apparently ten times more pleased.

Explanations followed on both sides.

"To think of your being stationed at Wingate!" exclaimed Cleopatra.

"But I am not stationed here, only passing through."

"Is there trouble with the White Mountain Apaches?"

"No. I told you that I had been ordered West, but did not explain in what capacity. I have been detailed to assist Captain Pratt at the Government Training School for Indians at Carlisle, Pennsylvania, and have been sent West to collect pupils."

There were some Zuñi Indians of a most unintellectual aspect hanging about the post. Madeleine was particularly disgusted by their lanky matted locks and uncleanly appearance. "I do not think the Indians here as interesting as the prisoners we saw at Florida," she said.

"These are Pueblos," Captain Saunters replied; "and when you have seen more of them, I think you will confess that in spite of many repulsive features they are interesting. To-morrow I start by ambulance for Fort Defiance in the Navajo Reservation. Would you like to accompany the expedition?"

Cleopatra and Madeleine thought they would like it very much. So did the Major; but Mrs. Morse preferred to rest in her present comfortable quarters, and Yulee decided that she would rather remain with her. The Captain, to Madeleine's surprise, made no effort to induce her to change her decision. "Some lover's quarrel," thought Madeleine; and she remonstrated with Yulee privately that night.

"I no like to see wild Indian," she said; "zat way I something like Mr. Hurlburt."

A ZUNI INDIAN.

It was the first time that the girl had mentioned his name, and she blushed as she did so. Madeleine was incensed. "Yulee," she said, "I do think that you treat Captain Saunters very shabbily, and I am quite vexed with you."

The girl's great pupils dilated with wonder. "It is nossing to Captain Saunters how I do treat him," she said.

"Nothing? Do you mean to say that you are not engaged to be married to him after your graduation at Vassar?"

Yulee laughed merrily. "Zat cannot be for two reason," she said; "for first I do not lofe him, and for twice he haf not ask me."

The ground seemed to swim beneath Madeleine; she walked away in a dazed condition. If Yulee and the Captain were not betrothed, there was no reason why Mr. Hurlburt should be unhappy. What had she done? It was late, and they were to start on their all-day's ambulance drive at dawn the next morning; but she sat up late to write a long letter to Mr. Hurlburt, explaining the misapprehension under which she had labored. "I may die on the trip," she said, when Cleopatra called to her sleepily to put off her letter-writing until their return from Defiance. Her new motto, "The most important duties first," was ringing in her ears, and to right this wrong was surely most important.

Sleepy, but with an appeased conscience, she roused herself the next morning for the jaunt across the wild prairie. Their ambulance was drawn by four stout mules, and another team brought equipage

THE NEVADA FALL IN THE [...]

and escort. It was a ride across a rolling prairie, gullied with numerous "aroyas," or gulches, treeless except for the scattered clumps of pinyon-trees, with only a prairie-dog town, or some strange flower like the yucca or Mexican soap-plant to relieve the monotony of the scene. Near Wingate, however, they had seen that strange rocky pinnacle called the Navajo Church; and if there had been nothing but the flat prairie, they would have enjoyed it for its very contrast to the cañons. They were mountain-tired. Their eyes as well as feet had had enough of climbing for the present; and the vast, sweeping, horizontal lines were restfully suggestive of plenty of room in which to lie down.

Fort Defiance they found a lonely outpost in the great Navajo reservation. The office of the agent, the store of the trader, a few houses belonging to the surgeon and other Government officials, and a school made up the sum total of the settlement.

Scattered about on the mesa in the vicinity were a few "hogans," or huts, of the Navajos, which showed commendable efforts on the part of the Indians toward living a civilized life. In one of them they saw a woman patiently working a worn-out sewing-machine. In a little arbor connected with another was a cooking-stove, and the owner had just taken out a pan of nice-looking biscuit. In several were looms upon which the occupants were weaving the beautiful blankets for which this nation is celebrated. The tribe raise vast flocks of sheep, and from their wool manufacture blankets so closely woven that they will hold water, and gayly striped and checkered in brilliant colors. They are of various sizes, from a saddle-cloth to a carpet; and Madeleine bought two for portières.

The Navajos are silversmiths also, and are peaceable, self-supporting Indians, not depending on the Government for rations, but farming their poor lands in many instances, and raising stock where the soil is only capable of grazing purposes.

The Navajo children are docile and bright, and anxious to array themselves in the white man's clothes, whenever they can obtain them. One fond mother had bartered a blanket which it had taken her several months to weave for a second-hand vest, a battered stovepipe hat, and a few cotton shirts for her eldest son, rather curiously

MADELEINE AND "HE-WANTS-TO-KNOW."

named "He-wants-to-know." He had attended school during one winter; and Madeleine presented him with a new geography which the teacher said he was anxious to obtain, and which was filled with pictures of the white man's inventions, of towns and railroads and farming implements, all strange and stimulating to his inquisitive mind.

His expression for a steamboat was a long compound word of his own invention, made up in the following ingenious way: A wagon with him was a "wooden-horse," a locomotive an "iron-wooden-horse;" a steamboat he called a "water-iron-wooden-horse." His diminutives were equally amusing. He called a wheel-barrow "a son-of-a-wagon," a hatchet "the son-of-an-axe," and a pistol "the son-of-a-gun."

The teachers at the school said that the children were shy, but when once induced to attend school made remarkable progress.

The Captain completed his arrangements for the transfer of a number of pupils to the Training School, and the party returned on the following day to Wingate.

"The Government ought to compel the attendance of all Indian children on the schools provided," said the Major, "and the Indian problem would then be solved."

"Ah, that is the trouble!" said the Captain, with a sigh. "The Government has always managed the problem in a half-hearted way, which shows that it has no desire to solve it."

"Then it is left to individual effort," exclaimed Madeleine; "and it seems to me that all great enterprises have been accomplished in that way. I, for one, have made up my mind that in some way I shall devote my life to this great cause of Indian education."

Captain Saunters looked up; a swift, glad light spreading over his face. They were in the swaying, jolting ambulance. The Major, who sat beside the Captain, saw nothing; but both of the girls understood the look. It said as plainly as words could have done, "I have wondered how you would regard this change in my career,— from a soldier's to a teacher's life; and if you will only share it, no man upon God's earth will be more blessed than I."

Madeleine understood it, and thought to herself, "My dream was true; he cares for me, has cared for me all along, and not for Yulee."

And then she thought how differently she would have felt if Yulee had not cleared her mental spectacles the night before. "I should have thought him a contemptible flirt, a man who could not help making love to every girl he saw; and now—"

Cleopatra, looking from one to the other, thought with amused dismay, " He is going to propose, and she will accept him right here before us all; " and she rattled away, telling her merriest stories, furbishing up old puns and conundrums and inventing new ones, to avert so dire a calamity.

INDIAN RESERVATIONS.

CHAPTER XV.

THE PUEBLOS.

EAVING Fort Wingate, the party next visited some of the Pueblo Indians. The word "pueblo" signifies "town;" and these Indians are so called because they build houses sometimes three stories high and shaped like terraces or a flight of steps, the roof of one house serving as front yard or veranda for the one above. These towns are very old. The early Franciscan missionaries found them, in 1583, looking just as they do now. They found the people partly civilized, practising the useful arts in a rude way, making several kinds of pottery, weaving, using wagons and farming implements, working in metals, constructing buildings and cisterns and ovens, and with a system of government and laws which proved them far advanced beyond the roving tribes of the plains; and all this before the Pilgrims landed on Plymouth Rock. There are nineteen of these towns. An account of these early discoveries of the Spaniards was printed in Madrid in 1586.

The ancient chronicler quaintly tells how the Franciscan, moved by a zeal for souls, made his first unsuccessful expedition into the new country, which he was obliged to abandon on account of the cowardice of his escort; and how, two years later, Antonio de Espeja, a wealthy gentleman from Cordova, invested a large part of his fortune in the fitting out of a stronger party, which successfully accomplished the exploration of New Mexico. Much that is written of this visit in 1583 is true to-day. In the old history the pueblo of Zuñi is described to the life, the Moqui villages can be recognized, and the Rio Grande pueblos can be traced from Acoma, on the west of the river, to Taos in the north, not far from the Colorado line.

The party found the Indians as hospitable, as simple in their habits, as ignorant of the outside world, as contented, and as inoffensive as Espeja found them. It is possible that they were more keenly struck by the picturesqueness and a certain foreignness than were the old Spaniards: for the adobe houses resembled those of the Moors, with which the explorers must have been familiar, and the narrow streets, with their unchristian odors, bear a striking resemblance to the towns of Morocco at the present day.

Our friends halted first at Laguna; and the Captain had arranged to reach the town on the annual feast-day, which is celebrated by a harvest dance. The Pueblos[1] have been Catholics ever since the coming of the Spaniards. An adobe church was the most striking of the buildings at Laguna; and stepping inside, the girls were shown an altar-piece painted upon skins, and brought many years before from Mexico. The ceremonies of the day were partly religious, the priest with his Indian altar-boys heading the procession and bearing the sacred images and banners from the church to an arbor constructed of corn-stalks, where the feast was held. As the day was the festival of Saint Joseph, an image of that saint was given the place of honor; his spouse, Maria Sanctissima, taking a more humble place. Upon the ground fruit and bread were piled, and the aged and honored members of the tribe took seats along the sides of the arbor. Then the people swarmed in; and the feast, a humble one, took place.

After the feast came the dance, which in this instance resembles an old-fashioned Virginia Reel, — with this important difference, that the woman must always keep her face to the back of her partner, the man.

[1] The word "Pueblo," as explained on the preceding page, is applied either to the towns or to the Indians themselves.

A ZUÑI VILLAGE.

One prominent feature of the day was the review of a mounted company of troops formed of Pueblo Indians, commanded by a white settler who has enlisted them into the United States service, and has drilled them with great zeal and patience. Twelve such companies of militia have been formed in New Mexico. The advance which this pueblo shows over some of the others is doubtless owing to the fact of the presence among them of American missionaries, — teachers and leaders, who have devoted themselves to their improvement. The gradual change of character in the ceremonies of their feast-day, the substitution of military evolutions for the war dance, pure and simple, and the absence of the old fetiches, show the progress of the people. In Zuñi, instead of the Roman Catholic emblems, the sacred animals of the old zoötheistic mythology (or beast-gods) are brought forward and receive the honors of the festival days.

The Major described a Rain Dance of the Zuñis, which he had seen. "Six mud images," said he, — "representing, as they told me, two bears, a deer, two rabbits, and a wolf, though I could hardly tell which was which, — were placed by a set of painted rascals in the centre of the plaza. Then the rest of the tribe danced around them, sprinkling them with prayer-meal until some hoodlums in masks rushed forward and shot the images. Then the painted fellows, who it seems were big medicine men, took up the pieces of the images and made a great howling over them, and the thing was over. They said they were dancing to make rain, but I could n't see any rhyme or reason in the ceremonies."

THE MAJOR.

"Speaking of dances," said the Captain, "the Moquis have a very disagreeable Snake Dance, which I once saw at the village of Wolpi.

This town is situated on a high cliff. For four days before the carnival the Indians occupied themselves in catching rattlesnakes. Some two hundred of these were collected and wrapped in withes and buffalo hide. The dance took place on the 18th of August, on the edge of the cliff. The dancers were painted grotesquely, and from the writhing, hydra-headed mass each, as he passed, was handed a serpent, which he seized in the middle with his teeth; and for half an hour the company danced in a circle, the snakes waving about their faces and seemingly about to bury their fangs in their throats, while the ground at their feet swarmed with other serpents. At the conclusion of this hideous orgy, the snakes were all gathered up by the dancers, who dashed at full speed down the precipitous rocks, and separating into four bands bounded away over the prairie toward the four points of the compass. When nearly out of sight, they set free the serpents, and returning disappeared into the estufa, or underground council-chamber. Apparently no one was harmed by the reptiles, whose bite is usually so dangerous. The meaning of this dance has not been explained."

At Laguna, through the kindness of the Governor of the pueblo, the party obtained conveyances, and drove over to the Indian town of Acoma, doubtless the most interesting and picturesque of all the pueblos. Like Wolpi, it is situated on a rocky cliff which rises abruptly from the plain. The children came running out to meet them, and guided them up the rocky defile, which was the only entrance to the citadel. The Governor made them a speech of welcome, and conducted them to the vacant cloisters of the little monastery, or mission-house connected with the church, explaining by expressive gestures that this was at their service so long as they cared to remain. Then he despatched a fleet courier fifteen miles for an interpreter, that he might learn the business of his guests. But before the arrival of the interpreter the hospitable people spread a table with all that it was in their power to offer, — jerked beef stewed with onions and

A ROOM IN THE PUEBLO OF ACOMA

plentifully seasoned with Chili or red pepper, bread baked in their mud ovens sprinkled with salt from a salt lake, eggs, black coffee, melons, and luscious peaches. Our travellers were hungry, and despite the absence of napery and finger-bowls, they made a good meal. After supper they strolled about the town, and examined the great cisterns, and the *campo santo*, or burial-ground, made on the face of the bare rock by bringing up the earth from the plain below in baskets. They saw the ponies and donkeys driven from their pastures up the rocky staircase and corralled for the night; and as the stars came out and they overlooked the town from the priest's balcony, the Captain read from his note-book a part of the relation of the friar Augustin Ryz, of which we have already spoken : —

"They found a great towne called Acoma, conteining above five thousand persons, situate upon an high rocke. The chief men of this towne came peaceably to visit the Spaniards, bringing them great plenty of victuals. Our men remained in this place three days, upon one of which the inhabitants made before them a very solemne dance, — using very witty sports wherewith our men were exceedingly delighted."

"Why, it seems exactly as if it were written of them to-day," exclaimed Madeleine.

"And to think," added Cleopatra, "that in all these years they have not outlived their childlike trustfulness, and receive us in the same hospitable manner, although they do not know our errand."

When the interpreter arrived, and the people understood that the party represented the Carlisle School, they were delighted. Many of them had relatives there; they crowded around to see the photographs of the buildings and of the pupils. picking out their friends, and testified their pleasure in every possible manner. They were eager to send more; and before the Captain had made the rounds of the pueblos, more children desirous of being taken had collected than could be received under the rules of the institution.

As the party were about leaving Acoma, Madeleine exclaimed, "I must have a flower from the cloister garden to press as a souvenir;" and she ran back to the neglected little patio, which had once blossomed so profusely under the tillage of the Franciscan Fathers. A yucca shot up a fountain-like spray in the centre of the court, and Madeleine plucked a blossom. As she did so, a young woman came in and threw her arms around her, embracing her with great tenderness and at the same time with great respect. The Captain followed her. "What does she say?" asked Madeleine, for the girl was talking excitedly.

"She apparently thinks," replied the Captain, "that you are one of the teachers at the Training School, and is thanking you for all you have done."

"I accept her thanks in advance," said Madeleine, "for what I mean to do. See, I have plucked a yucca-blossom, such as they use to cleanse their blankets with. It shall be for me the emblem of cleansing. Do you know that beautiful Spanish song, —

THE INTERPRETER.

> 'I'll weary myself by night and by day
> To aid my unfortunate brothers,
> As the laundress tans her own face in the ray
> To cleanse the garments of others'?"

And the Captain — Well, no, we will not tell what he said; but as they came out of the cloister garden into the cool quiet church, they paused before the altar, where a single light was burning, and holding each other's hands pledged themselves, as they afterward repeated the vow in another sanctuary, " each to the other and both to God."

CHAPTER XVI.

TAKEN PRISONER.

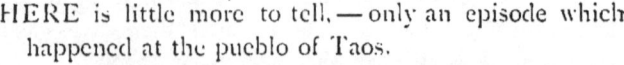HERE is little more to tell,—only an episode which happened at the pueblo of Taos.

They had gone thither on the 30th of September to witness the festival of San Geronimo, which is celebrated here with races and old pagan ceremonies, mingled with the rites of the Roman Catholic Church. It was their last stop, and it rounded up the circle of their Western tour; for Taos is not far from Colorado Springs, where they may be said to have begun their Western wanderings. It lies away from the railroad, is difficult of access to travellers, and the fête has been witnessed by few tourists.

The old Mexican town of Fernandez de Taos is situated about two miles from the Indian pueblo. The town has the appearance of a citadel, and has so figured in history; for the warriors of Taos are noted among the pueblos for their bravery, and for a certain rash espousal of the under side in a fight, never knowing when they are beaten, but sustaining sieges and winning battles after the general surrender. It was here that Popé originated the rebellion and drove the Spaniards from the country in 1680, sending about to the other Indians a rope containing as many knots as there were pueblos. Each pueblo that joined the revolt untied a knot, and when the rope was returned the number of insurgent towns was known. All rose except the little pueblo of St. Juan, which was rechristened by the Spaniards on their return, in 1693, St. Juan de los Caballeros.

"In 1848," said the Major, "Taos, which had led the rebellion against the Mexicans in former days, was the only pueblo that sided

ANCIENT PUEBLO RESTORED.

with them in their ineffectual struggle with the United States. Led by the warrior Tomas, it sustained a two days' artillery siege, the howitzers playing without effect on the thick walls of the adobe church. I was a lieutenant under General Cooke, who led this assault. I have often heard him speak of the soldierly qualities of these Indians with enthusiasm, and he told me that seven years later he raised here in a day a company to serve against the Apaches, and his expression was, ' Efficient fine fellows they were!'" Kit Carson, the famous pioneer and Indian fighter, is buried at Fernandez de Taos; and the party stopped here to visit his grave. This delay had a rather curious effect.

It so happened that news of their coming reached Taos, handed from the Indians of one pueblo to another, before their own arrival. Now, this is one of the most conservative of the pueblos. Their old civilization these Indians consider good enough for them; and they cling more tenaciously than any others, unless it be the Zuñis, to the old pagan legends, and especially to the beautiful one of Montezuma, their hero god. Long, long ago, Montezuma, so the legend runs, left his children to journey toward the east, leaving them word to kindle beacon-fires at sunrise, for at that hour some morning he would return. It is said that among these northern pueblos the fires are still kindled, and the chiefs watch at sunrise for the return of Montezuma. One of the Taos chief men who had long pondered over this promise of the return of Montezuma, hearing that a man was coming who desired to educate and benefit the pueblo children, became impressed with the idea that this was possibly Montezuma. His associates scoffed at the notion; but from constantly brooding upon it the poor old man became more and more eager, and anxious lest Taos should be passed by. He was fiscal of police, and he sent a body-guard of stout young warriors out on the road by which he expected the celestial visitant, to intercept him and bring him perforce to the city.

When, a day or two before the festival, the party reached Taos, the very first person whom they met on entering the town proved to be an old friend. Madeleine uttered a little scream of delighted surprise, and Yulee turned first pale and then rosy; for there, with knapsack and staff, talking with the aged fiscal, was Mr. Hurlburt. He hurried forward to meet them, his first impulse of happiness carrying him beyond the feeling of restraint which the sight of Yulee would have caused had he given himself time to think.

"I have had the strangest experience," he exclaimed. "I have been prospecting in the mountains. You see, after our outing in the Yellowstone, I did not feel like cooping myself up in an office, and I had heard of some turquoise and silver mines in this vicinity that were worked by the old Spaniards. I had been roughing it with two companions; but discouraged by our poor success they left me, and I decided to give up the search and make for some point on the Denver and Rio Grande Railroad. When a short distance from this place, I was met by a mounted party of Indians, surrounded and brought a prisoner into Taos. As I was single-handed, I thought best from the first not to show fight; but I assure you I was frightened. I said to myself, 'If Miss Morse could see me now, she might change her opinion of the Indians.' I expected nothing less than death, and perhaps torture, and concluded I was to be served up to grace the games of their festal day, which I knew was approaching. What was my astonishment, on my arrival here, at being greeted in a cordial manner by this venerable party, who explained through an interpreter that he had heard of my kind thoughts and feelings toward Indians, and desired to do me honor."

MR. HURLBURT AS A PROSPECTOR.

Cleopatra laughed. "You must have thought that he was indulging in mild satire," she said.

"So I did, until others of the Indians explained that the fame of the Government schools at Carlisle and Hampton had reached them, and that I was supposed to be in some way connected with them, and they wished to share in the benefits of these admirable institutions. If I was surprised before, I was thunderstruck now. I never had heard of Indians wishing to share in anything connected with civilization, with the exception of whiskey, and it seemed to me that either I or they had gone crazy. I still believe that the old gentleman here is a little shaky in his mind, for he evidently thinks that Captain Pratt is Montezuma come again; but the rest of the community seem to be level-headed, except in the notion that the Government cares enough for them to send any one to look after their children."

"They are correct in that idea, my friend," replied the Major. "Allow me to introduce Captain Saunters, who is here on this very errand, and for whom you were mistaken."

Mr. Hurlburt and the Captain greeted each other cordially, and some kindly but earnest chat followed on the question of Indian education. "I have gained a new respect for Indians," said Mr. Hurlburt; "and my prejudice has been based on this fact, that in some tribes missionaries have been working for years without any adequate result, and I have known of one or two instances where Indian boys educated in the East, after they returned to their tribes, went back to a wild way of living."

"That is the mistake we make," replied the Captain, warmly. "We educate one Indian out of a thousand, and demand that he civilize his tribe single-handed, with all the overpowering weight of barbaric surroundings against him. The Government should compel the education of *all* these wild wards, and then allow them to become absorbed, scattered among our people, their tribe forgotten, swallowed up in the great American nation. We have been acting on the plan of isolating one missionary among a thousand Indians;

we must isolate each Indian among a thousand missionaries, and then we may hope for success."

The party found the festival most interesting. The morning witnessed every available roof covered with a swarm of gayly blanketed spectators, who had come in from all the country round to witness the sports. Fruit-venders at little stalls, and panier-laden donkeys added bright spots of color. Pony and foot races, and a service in the church filled the morning. The afternoon was given up to dances. In one, the Cold Weather Dance, the men were dressed

WATCHING A PUEBLO DANCE.

to represent great poverty. Their hats were horned and tasselled with corn-husks; and other allusions were made to the harvest season, and their needs for the approaching winter. Some went through the motions of cutting wood; others sawed and threw it into piles. The women, wearing each two blankets to represent the severity of the weather, followed, and enacted the picking up of the wood; and the dance ended about an imaginary fire.

It was while looking on at this dance that Madeleine asked Mr. Hurlburt if he had received her letter from Wingate, and learning that he had not, told him of her great mistake in regard to Yulee.

"I will forgive you," said the young man, "if she will forgive me, and if you will help me to persuade her to become a miner's wife."

No great persuasion was necessary, for Yulee's heart had long been given; and when she learned that her birth had nothing to do with her lover's estrangement, her wounded pride was soothed and all was happily settled. Yulee's only stipulation was that she should finish her scientific course at Vassar, and teach botany long enough to pay her indebtedness to her friends before her marriage.

It was in vain that Mr. Hurlburt desired to assume that indebtedness. Yulee, for once, was obstinate. She wanted her education, but not enough to sacrifice to it her womanly independence; and Mr. Hurlburt was forced very unwillingly to acquiesce.

It was time now for the girls to return to college. Their long tour together over thousands of miles of railroad was over. The intimacy of travel in comfortable and in trying situations had not caused them to weary of each other or brought out selfish or unlovely traits. Inconveniences had been laughed over, heat and weariness had been ignored, the jar of the rails had waked no answering thrill in quivering nerves, and good nature had been the buffer in every mental collision. That they were glad to return to Vassar was only a proof, as Cleopatra said, not that they loved railroading less, but that they loved their college more.

After passing her examinations it was discovered that Yulee's proficiency in botany was such that she could act as assistant in that department, and so pay her own expenses. Madeleine would have been disappointed but for Yulee's evident delight, and for the knowledge that this would shorten the engagement which had seemed so long to Mr. Hurlburt.

Aunt Pen, on hearing of Madeleine's betrothal to Captain Saunters, took all the credit to herself for having brought it about, and busied herself with great interest in preparing the trousseau. It was arranged that the double wedding should occur at Madeleine's home. Shy Raphael Ponce and his stately wife would be present. Cleopatra was to be bridesmaid; and after that would begin the true life of THREE VASSAR GIRLS AT HOME.

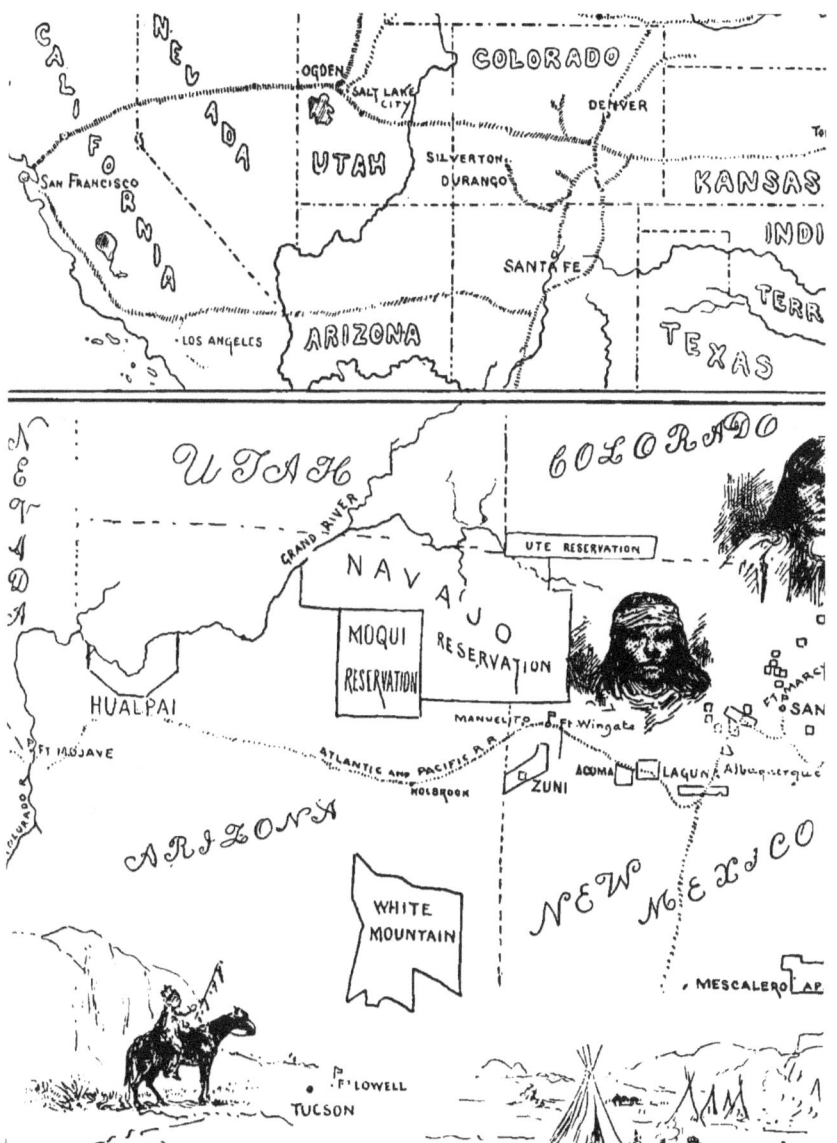

www.ingramcontent.com/pod-product-compliance
Lightning Source LLC
Chambersburg PA
CBHW021809230426
43669CB00008B/689